Find the Errors! II

PROOFREADING ACTIVITIES

Nancy Lobb

 WALCH PUBLISHING®

User's Guide
to
Walch Reproducible Books

Purchasers of this book are granted the right to reproduce all pages where this symbol appears.

This permission is limited to a single teacher, for classroom use only.

Any questions regarding this policy or requests to purchase further reproduction rights should be addressed to:

Permissions Editor
J. Weston Walch, Publisher
P.O. Box 658
Portland, Maine 04104-0658

1   2   3   4   5   6   7   8   9   10
ISBN 0-8251-4328-4

Contents

To the Teacher

How to Use This Book

Find the Errors! II is a sequel to the best-selling Walch publication *Find the Errors!* It is written on a slightly higher level than the original and contains more comprehensive treatment of grammar and style rules. *Find the Errors! II* gives students a chance to find and correct common writing errors in humorous anecdotes. Each of the 35 worksheets focuses on a particular kind of error, including spelling, punctuation, capitalization, grammar, usage, and correct sentence structure. By completing the exercises in these books, students will become more skilled at editing their own written work, thus producing a better final copy.

Find the Errors! II is a reproducible teacher book containing both student worksheets and teacher material. The reproducible student material includes 35 exercises, as well as a pretest and posttest on the contents of *Find the Errors! II*. Reproducible pages are identified by the copyright line with a flame logo at the bottom. They can be copied and distributed to each student. For each reproducible student page, information in the Teacher's Guide (page 40) provides background information on the topic presented, an answer key, and activities pertaining to that topic.

The Reproducible Student Exercises

Editing written work consists of two parts: (1) proofreading to find errors in spelling, punc-tuation, and capitalization and (2) editing for sense to ensure that the words and sentences are written in a way that conveys the intended meaning. *Find the Errors! II* contains exercises that relate to both of these topics.

Each exercise in *Find the Errors! II* also contains five spelling errors for students to locate and correct. The words chosen for this purpose are not long, difficult words. Rather they are common spelling errors made by many students. Each spelling word falls into one of three categories:

1. Words that are often confused, such as *your* and *you're*.

2. Words that illustrate basic spelling rules, such as *relieve* or *winning*.

3. Words taken from lists of "Spelling Demons," such as *tomorrow*.

The Pretest and Posttest

A pretest and posttest have been included for assessment. The pretest may be used to determine specific areas in which students have difficulty. It can also be used to help you focus on particular areas in which students need work.

Each item in the pretest and posttest contains one or more major writing errors. The errors in each sentence are identified and corre-lated with the appropriate student worksheet in the Answer Key on pages 52 and 67.

The Teacher's Guide

For each topic presented in *Find the Errors! II*, the Teacher's Guide presents background information, an answer key, and activities. The background information section includes a detailed explanation of the rules that are included in that writing skill area. The answer section contains the anecdote rewritten correctly, with corrected errors underlined. The activities section contains suggestions for teaching the lesson and expanding the concepts taught. Also, there are suggestions for teaching to different learning styles, cooperative learning, and multicultural activities.

Provision for Individual Differences

A section entitled "Using Your Learning Style for Better Proofreading" (p. *vii*) in the student introduction gives students suggested methods for more effective proofreading. Auditory, visual, and tactile learners are given specific suggestions on ways to use their particular learning strength to become better proofreaders.

The Proofreading Checklist

The Proofreading Checklist (p. *viii*) provides students with a useful guide to check their own writing errors. This tool may help students transfer the skills they have learned in *Find the Errors! II* to their own writing.

To the Student

Sharks Biting off the Coast of Virginia!

Falling Over the Cliff,
Photographer Shoots Waterfall!

There Will Be a Fair Increase on Tuseday!

The goal of writing is to communicate your ideas effectively. The sentences above do not reach this goal because of errors in spelling and sentence structure. Poor writing can cause lower grades in school, lack of advancement on the job, and social embarrassment.

It is important to proofread your written work to make sure you are communicating effectively. Proofreading consists of two parts. First, it means editing your work for sense. You must make sure that your words and sentences are saying what you want them to say. Secondly, proofreading means reading your work closely to find errors in spelling, punctuation, capitalization, grammar, and usage.

Using Your Learning Style for Better Proofreading

You can use your learning style to help you proofread your work more effectively. Here's how:

1. If you are primarily a visual learner, make it a practice to scan slowly everything you've written. You may wish to do this twice if it is an important piece of work such as a job application. Look at each word and be sure it's right!

2. If you are primarily an auditory learner, try reading your written work aloud as you proofread. This will help you focus your attention on your writing. Mistakes will jump into focus as you read the words aloud.

3. If you are primarily a tactile learner, try moving your finger under the words as you read them. Again, this will help you focus on each word.

You may find any or all of these ideas helpful to you. Try using one or more of these methods for proofreading your work. See what works best for you. Then make it a habit! Proofread all your written work carefully. You'll find it's not hard to eliminate careless errors from your written work. This will bring you rewards in school, on the job, and in social situations.

A word about the spell-checker on your personal computer. The spell-checker can be a useful tool for identifying errors. But, resist the temptation to rely on it completely. For example, the computer will not tell you that you typed *form* when you meant to type *from*. In the final analysis, the best proofreader of all is *YOU*.

Name _____   Date _____

Proofreading Checklist

Directions: Refer to this checklist for all of your written work. Check
the list to see that you have proofread well and have
caught all the errors.

I have checked to see that . . .

1. Capital letters are used whenever needed.

2. Commas are used only as necessary.

3. Direct quotations are enclosed in quotation marks.

4. Colons, hyphens, apostrophes, parentheses, and underlining (italics) are used where needed.

5. All subjects and verbs agree.

6. Correct principal parts of verbs are used.

7. Pronoun references are clear and correct.

8. Numbers and numerals are written correctly.

9. Abbreviations are written correctly.

10. There are no spelling or usage errors.

11. Dangling or misplaced modifiers have been corrected.

12. Run-on sentences and sentence fragments have been eliminated.

13. Sentences vary in length and form.

14. Verb tense is consistent throughout.

15. Wordy sentences have been simplified.

16. Interesting vocabulary has been used, instead of trite, nondescriptive words.

17. Comparisons have been made correctly.

18. This writing represents my best effort.

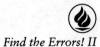

Name _____ Date _____

Find the Errors! II Pretest

Directions: Each sentence below has one or more errors. In the space below each sentence, rewrite the sentence correcting all errors. Circle the 10 misspelled words in the Pretest and spell them correctly when you rewrite the sentences. (Missing capital letters do not count as misspellings.)

---

1. Our american literature class visited rowan oak the oxford mississippi home of the well known writer william faulkner auther of the book *the sound and the fury.*

2. Our teacher mr. c j cobb jr told us that we would have a school holiday on columbus day and we all yelled Hooray!

3. On the biology exam the students grades included 8 As, 7 Bs, and 6 Cs however the teacher was not satisfied with they're performance.

4. The suspect was described as a 5'10" male with a heavy black mustache weighing 150 pounds.

5. Each of the three boys have his own bedroom which means they don't never fight.

6. Yoku went to the refrigerater sees it is empty and makes out a shopping list.

7. Reese is going to glacier national park where you can go hiking and fishing.

(continued)

Find the Errors! II Pretest *(continued)*

8. Keri and Ken like to cook, Especially on the weekends, When they have extra time.

9. The nile river is nearly 4,160 miles long, it is the longest river in the world.

10. Sojourner truth was born a slave. She was born in New York. She was born in the late 18th centery. She fought against slavery. She was anti-slavery.

    where

11. In the winter I enjoy winter sports such as skiing and ice skating when it is winter.

12. The teeth of a crocodile are sharper than a humans.

    of those of

13. Twelve-year-old Sara and her friends sat altogether at the movie, sharing a huge box of popcorn between them, talking alot and doing everything accept watching the movie.

    were sitting   *a lot*   *except*

14. She might of past the algebra exam, but she maybe in trouble with her science test, the reason is because she forgot about the later.

    may have passed   *may be*   *for*

15. Jens told his teacher mr. winfield that his dog ate his homework. When the teacher looked disbelieving jens said he didnt want to but I made him.

    appeared   *he*   *his dog*

1. Capital Letters I

Directions: Add capital letters where they are needed in the story. Circle the five misspelled words. Write them correctly in the Spelling Box.

Two friends, han and jed, from boston, massachusetts, planned a trip together every spring break. One year they went to orlando, florida, where they stayed at the disney hotel and enjoyed disney world for three days. Another year they went to new york city, where they saw the play *hamlet,* ate in the restaurant the four seasons, and visited the empire state building. This year for a change they decided to go camping in the rocky mountains of montana.

From l.l. green company, they purchased a two-man dome tent that had been highly rated by *consumer reports* magazine. They bought coleman sleeping bags and swiss army knives. The rest of their equipment they were able to borrow from jed's dad. They pored over the guidebook *camping in the wilds* by n.a. tent for advise on making the trip more fun.

On saturday, march 15, spring break began. The boys climbed into their old volkswagen van to begin the drive. By driving all night, they were able to arrive at clark's fork of the yellow-stone river by monday. They pitched their tent and made camp.

The boys began to do some fly-fishing for rainbow trout. It wasn't long before they noticed the huge mosquitos swarming about. "They're as big as b-1 bombers," jed cried, applying a heavy dose of off insectiside.

"No, more like the concorde," han replied. "By the way, did you know that the cheif enemy of the mosquito is fish like the brown, rainbow, and cutthroat trout?"

After a delicious meal of fried trout and beanie weenies, the boys decided to call it a day. They carefully adjusted their repel brand mosquito netting and climbed into their bags. Nonetheless, a number of intrepid mosquitoes found them. A spraying of insecticide finally abatted the attack. A few minutes later, han noticed some fireflies.

He said to his friend, "we might as well give up, jed; those mosquitoes are looking for us with flashlights now!"

SPELLING BOX	1. _____	2. _____
3. _____	4. _____	5. _____

Name _____ Date _____

2. Capital Letters II

Directions: Add capital letters where they are needed in the story. Circle the five misspelled words. Rewrite them correctly in the Spelling Box.

judie was attending a christmas party at the home of dr. c. j. cobb, mayer of hazlehurst, alabama. It was the saturday before christmas, and judie had attended a number of lavish affairs, one with mexican food, one with italian food, and another with traditional american food. judie now had an extra ten pounds to show for it.

judie struck up a conversation with a young woman named ila m. slim. ila, a graduate of alabama state, began talking about her job. "you know, it's sad," she said. "so many people these days are out of work, and here i am living off the fat of the land."

"how do you do that?" judie asked.

"i'm an aerobics instructer at webster's gym in the sears building," she replied. "come join us in january. we are starting a new aerobics group."

judie was afraid she would look huge among all the svelte women wearing their spandex speedo workout clothes. But she had made a new year's resolution to lose wait. So on january 2, she hopped in her toyota and took highway 51 to webster's gym.

arriving at the gym, she chose an acme treadmill in the far west corner of the room, hoping to be inconspicuous. she worked out for ten minutes. then ila arrived, put on a tape of "go you chicken fat, go," and began the 60-minute workout.

judie tried to keep up, but fell farther and farther behind. It had been a long time since she had taken body conditioning 101 at hendrix college. She saw one person after another turn and stair at her. She hoped it was just her imagination. She tried to imagine herself somewhere else, like in the rocky mountains listening to mozart. But when one woman turned, stared at her, and squinted to get a better look, Judie wanted to disapear.

judie stopped her workout and picked up her nike duffel bag. She hoped to sneak undetected out the west door, which led to the high street parking lot, and make a swift getaway in her camry. As she turned, she realized that the gym's only wall clock, a small nine-inch elgin, had been hanging just inches above her head the entire time.

SPELLING BOX	1. _____	2. _____
3. _____	4. _____	5. _____

3. Commas I

Directions: Add commas where they are needed. Do not add any unnecessary commas. Circle the five misspelled words. Write them correctly in the Spelling Box.

January 25 20—

Dear Dad

Yes things are going well at school but they could be better. Last weekend I took Sue out to dinner the dance and a movie. My suit was wrinkled and I had to take it to the cleaners. We tried that cozy quaint restaurant you mentioned. It was good but expensive. Sue ordered not surprisingly the most expensive entrée on the menu. You did say to treat her well didn't you?

On Tuesday January 14 I got repairs done on my car. I took it to the shop you recomended at 145 Kings Highway Bangor Maine. Dad it cost fifty dollars for the belts fifty dollars for laber and another twenty for the oil change. After looking it over the mechanic Keith Crenshaw said the car is shot. Alarmed by the many things wrong he fixed only the most essenshul. Well you can guess what I really need. I hope you will send some soon.

Your son

Miguel Olmos Jr.

January 30 20—

Dear Son

Nothing pleases me more than a letter from Northern Maine University. I know you are getting a great education and the ability to solve problems independintly. Oh I guess you are a chip off the old block aren't you?

Well nothing much is going on around here. It is all most noon and your sister is still in bed. No one is awake but me. There is no time like the present to give this letter to the mailman who will send it your way.

Your dad

Miguel Olmos Sr.

SPELLING BOX	1. _____	2. _____
3. _____	4. _____	5. _____

4. Commas II

Directions: Add commas where they are needed in the story. Do not add any unnecessary commas. Circle the five misspelled words. Rewrite them correctly in the Spelling Box.

Jay had been fishing for walleye his favorite fish at a remote lake in Wisconsin all week and he had had little sucess. He had tried minnows lures and jigs all to no avail. It had been most discouraging so he was thinking about packing up and heading for home.

That afternoon he saw a fisherman standing in the lake holding a mirror. Attached to the handle of the mirror was a large net. "Excuse me" Jay said "but what are you doing?"

"I'm fishing of coarse" came the reply.

"With a mirror?" Jay asked thinking the man was crazy.

"Yep it's my latest invention and this time I'm going to make a fortune!" the man said.

"How does it work?" Jay asked already smelling a fish fry.

"Well I'll tell you but it will cost you $100" the man said appearing reluctant to share his secret.

Jay was anxious to catch some fish to take home so he reached in his pocket counted out the money and handed it to the man.

"O.K." the fisherman said. "You aim the mirror into the water and when the fish swims by the rays of light reflected from the mirror shine right in his eyes. This temperarily blinds the fish and he begins to swim in a circle in confushun. Then you simply dip the net into the water and you grab him with it."

"Oh that's the dumbest thing I've ever heard! How many have you caught like this?"

"Well you're the third one today!" answered the fisherman with a smile.

SPELLING BOX	1. _____	2. _____
3. _____	4. _____	5. _____

5. Quotation Marks

Directions: Add quotation marks, single quotation marks, and other punctuation marks where they are needed. Circle the five misspelled words. Write them correctly in the Spelling Box.

A nervous, balding man in his 40's had an apointment to see a councilor. He had never gotten help before, but he told himself that things were so bad he had to do something! He pulled into the parking lot, ignoring the sign that read Exit Only. The theme song Titanic was going around in his head. I'm really losing it he told himself with a sinking feeling.

I'm supposed to go to the door with a sign that says Dr. Lucy D. Hope, Therapist, he reminded himself. She told me on the phone You can't miss it.

Finding the office an hour later, the man was relieved. It's a good thing I aloud plenty of time; I'm not even late! he told himself.

Dr. Hope ushered him into her comfortable office. What seems to be the problem she asked.

Doctor, I just don't know what to do! Its all more than I can stand he began.

Well, just calm down and tell me all about it she replied. As I always say A burden shared is a burden lightened.

O.K., Doctor. I have a five-bedroom home on three acres on Lake Caroline in Madison County. I drive a BMW and my wife drives a Jaguar. I have three children in college, and I bought each of them a new car. We belong to the country club. Each summer we spend a month in Europe.

Haven't you ever heard the expression it's not nice to brag said the counselor. Let's get back to what is really bothering you.

Don't you see the man shouted. I only make $700 a month!

SPELLING BOX	1. _____	2. _____
3. _____	4. _____	5. _____

6. Hyphens, Colons, and Semicolons

Directions: Add semicolons, hyphens, and colons where they are needed. Circle the five misspelled words. Write them correctly in the Spelling Box.

It was a rainy looking day the five year old boy couldn't find anything to do. His mother suggested the following video games, coloring, helping in the kitchen, and playing "hide and seek." None of these activities intrested the boy everything was "boring." It was only 10 30 A.M., and the forecast was for all day thunderstorms. Thunder and lightening, as well as torrents of rain, were coming down from dark looking clouds.

Finally, the mother hit on a plan. She pulled a well worn photo album from the shelf. She began showing the boy pictures of long forgoten times.

"Here is your Uncle Fred. A self made man, he was well liked by everyone. And here is Aunt Josie on the day she turned twenty one. Here is your great grandmother reading her favrite Bible verse, John 3 16. There are many more pictures here of your brothers, sisters, and other family members. I need to go put the roast in the oven however, I'll be back in about 10 minutes."

The little boy continued looking through the album. When he was about three fourths done, he saw someone he didn't reconize.

"Mom," he called. "Who is this red headed man standing next to Ahn? You know, the curly haired one with the funny looking glasses?"

"Why, that's your hard working father you know that!" exclaimed his mother.

The boy spent nearly one half minute puzzling over this all perplexing problem however, he was still confused.

"But, Mom," he replied. "If that's Dad, who's that bald headed man upstairs?"

SPELLING BOX	1. _____	2. _____
3. _____	4. _____	5. _____

Find the Errors! II

7. Apostrophes

Directions: Add apostrophes where they are needed in the story. Circle the five misspelled words. Write them correctly in the Spelling Box.

Revel Applewhite was a mechanic at Wongs Automotive. Ten years experience and careful attention to his customers needs, always minding his *p*s and *q*s, had made him the subject of many customers requests. He even worked on his mother-in-laws car to her satisfaction. Its hard to meet everyones needs all of the time, but Revel gave it his best shot. He still tells the story of the hard-to-please customer he met in January 03.

Mr. Ortiz brought in his twin daughters car to be repaired. He told the mechanic, "Its making a very strange noise, then its stalling."

Revel took the girls car into his shop. He started the motor and listened to its sound. It would run smoothly for about thirty seconds time, then stall. Its stalling did not puzzle Revel at all. He took out a small hammar and tapped the engine three times lightly in the same spot. Once again he started the moter and listened to its sound. "Well, its fixed. Ill mail you a bill," he told Mr. Ortiz.

Two days later, Mr. Ortiz opened the bill from Wongs Automotive. It read:

> For taping engine with hammer: $1
>
> For knowing where to tap: $1,000
>
> Total: $1001

Mr. Ortiz blood pressure went through the roof. He called Revel to make his complants. "There are too many *0*s in this bill! I never heard of such prices since back in 01! Itll be a cold day in July before Ill take my car back to your shop. Id have replaced the childrens car before Id have agreed to spend all that! Thats a week of my pay!"

"Well, if the cars stalling has stopped, the piece of mind should be worth it," Revel replied, accepting the stack of hundreds with a smile.

SPELLING BOX	1. _____	2. _____
3. _____	4. _____	5. _____

Find the Errors! II

Name _____   Date _____

8. Parentheses

Directions: Add parentheses and punctuation marks where they are needed in the story. Circle the five misspelled words. Write them correctly in the Spelling Box.

A local camping goods store this large store sells goods for camping in all types of climates and terrain conducted camping workshops every Monday. One week the topic was "Climbing the Himalayas" a mountain range in southern Asia. Another week the topic was "Whitewater Rafting in Mississippi" Mississippi is principly known for its slow-moving creeks, so this topic generated a good deal of curiosity. "Hiking in the Artic" was another popular lecture. This Monday July 16 the topic for the workshop was "Dessert Survival." A large group of prospective campers they ranged in age from 16 to 60 assembled in the store at 7:00 P.M for the ocasion.

"What are the three most important things you should bring with you put them in order of their importance in case you get lost in the desert?" the leader asked.

A lot of discussion some of it was pretty heated ensued. Everyone seemed to have strong opinions. Finally the group at least most of them reached a consensus.

"A compass, a canteen of water, and a deck of cards," answered the spokesperson the most experienced camper.

"Please explain your choices aren't your prioritys strange?" the leader replied.

"The compass as I am sure anyone would know is to find in which direction you should go. A compass it is an instrument with a needle that points to the magnetic north pole is easy to carry in your pocket. After all it's pretty easy to get lost in the desert with so few landmarks to go by. A canteen of water you can survive only a short time without water, while you can live weeks without food would be vital this would be to prevent dehydration," was the reply.

"What about the deck of cards an odd idea?" the leader persisted.

"Well, as soon as you start playing solitaire which would be a good way to relax after a long day of trudging through the sand someone is sure to come up behind you and say, 'Put that black ten on the red jack!' And then you're found!"

SPELLING BOX	1. _____	2. _____
3. _____	4. _____	5. _____

9. Italics, Underlining, and Quotation Marks

Directions: Add underlining (italics), quotation marks, and single quotation marks where they are needed in the story. Circle the five misspelled words. Write them correctly in the Spelling Box.

Mrs. Moore's English class was discussing their favrite works of art and litrature. It was a livly discussion with everyone in the class participating.

"My favorite painting is Physical Education by Jim Shorts," said Shay.

"I heard a great song called Garden Mulch by the group Peat Moss," said Mary.

"I saw an exciting action movie called Runaway Train last weekend," added Mario. "It was directed by Dee Rail."

Tran raised his hand. "The poem Why Dogs Scratch by Manny Fleas is hilarious," he said.

Alex mentioned that his dad had bought a new cookbook called The Cookout Cookbook by Burntoo A. Crisp.

"There was a terrific article in the magazine Sports Pictured. It was called How to Be Great at Sports by Hugh Da Mann!" offered Tony.

"You know how I love to watch ads on television," Akira broke in. "Well, on Tuesday I saw this great television special called Classic Comercials, directed by Will B. Wrightback."

Gavin said that in the newspaper The Jackson Times he had read an article called Proof-reading by the famous writer Ty Poe.

The teacher called the class to order. "I think I'll take a week off. I've been reading the article Planing a Vacation by Vera U. Going and I think I'm ready for a break. Remember, your book reports are due next week. You will find an excellent resource guide in the book Need Help Writing a Book Report? by Philip A. Page. I hope you have a great week with the substitute, Mrs. A. Skeeme. She'll probably fill you all in on the book she's writing called How to Make Money Easily."

SPELLING BOX	1. _____	2. _____
3. _____	4. _____	5. _____

10. Numbers and Numerals

Directions: Rewrite each sentence below, correcting any errors with numbers or numerals. If a sentence has no errors, write CORRECT. Circle the five misspelled words. Write them correctly in the Spelling Box.

1. "At 5:00 I asked you to notise when the 16-Bean Soup boiled over."

   "I did, Mom! It boiled over at six fifteen P.M. on October Twenty, 2004.

2. "Let's say I take 7 apples from twelve apples. What's the diffrence?"

   "That's what I say: What's the difrence?"

3. "Why should the number two hunderd eighty eight never be mentioned in polite company?"

   "Because it is two gross." (A gross is 144.)

4. "Mr. Green is a butcher who lives in Apartment Eight C at 1453 North Sixty-Sixth Street. His shop is at 15 2nd Avenue. He is 40 years old, six feet tall and wears a size eleven shue. What does he weigh?"

   "Meat."

5. "What occurs one time in a minute, 2 times in a moment, but not once in the twenti-eth centery?"

   "The letter *m*."

6. "How are you doing training your new dog?"

   "Great! Yesterday I taught her to beg. Today she came back with 45 cents."

SPELLING BOX	1. _____	2. _____
3. _____	4. _____	5. _____

11. Abbreviations

Directions: Write the abbreviations for the italicized words or phrases in the following sentences. Circle the five misspelled words. Write them correctly in the Spelling Box.

1. In Dallas, *Texas* today, *Mister Abner Bart* Payton, *Junior,* District Director of the *Internal Revenue Service,* anounced a new nickname for the agency: "The Taxes Rangers."

2. At 8:00 *ante meridiem* the *Federal Bureau of Investigation* reported a leek in its Jackson, *Mississippi* Secret Affairs *Department* located at *North* Michigan *Avenue.* The entire *United States* was upset until it was revealed that the leek was in the men's room sink.

3. On the *American Broadcasting Company* news at 6:15 *post meridiem,* Professor *Ignatio Mergutroid* Windy, *Doctor of Philosophy* announced that there will be 200 million cars on the road by the year 2010. If anyone wants to cross Kings *Boulevard,* they'd better do it now!

4. *Sergeant Bill Adolphi* Hardguy yelled at *Private Ivan Mark* Timid, "Have you filled those salt shakers yet?"

   "No, sir! It's hard pushing the salt through those little wholes."

5. *Senator* Bigmouth, can you recite *Abraham* Lincoln's Gettysburg Address?"

   "No, but he used to live in the White House at 1600 Pennsylvania *Avenue* in Washington, *District of Columbia.*"

6. The teacher suspected that her class wasn't paying attention, so she lapsed into nonsence talk. "Take one *centimeter* of scrital, adding it carefully to a *gallon* of fendered asplat. Add two *pounds* of frittel and a *milligram* of ziffer. Are there any questions?"

   "Yes, what is ziffer?"

SPELLING BOX	1. _____	2. _____
3. _____	4. _____	5. _____

---

12. Review of Punctuation and Capitalization I

Directions: Add capital letters and punctuation marks where they are needed in the story. Circle the five misspelled words. Rewrite them correctly in the Spelling Box.

rodney and lindsey lived in palatka florida a small hamlet in the central part of the state. Since florida has a humid subtropical climate they were unaccustomed to snow ice and cold weather. Not once did they have to get up early to warm the car scrape ice off the windsheild or watch the weather report on television.

rodney was a twenty one year old self employed carpenter. Lindsey a recent high school graduate was a well liked teaching assistent in a local elementary school. Both liked their jobs however neither was well paid. They decided to apply for jobs in another state. At 10 30 a m on friday october 15 the mail arrived at their home at 125 athens ct palatka florida with exciting news. Both had job offers in buffalo new york a spot far distant from florida. Being adventurous they decided to take the jobs.

Soon after they arrived a big snowstorm hit buffalo. being on the shore of lake erie buffalo is subject to a phenomenon known not surprisingly as the lake effect. Winds blow over the lake picking up moisture. Hitting the shore they dump unusually large amounts of precipitation rain or snow on the city. This particular storm dumped nearly two feet of snow on the newcomers home.

The next morning as lindsey was backing out of the driveway her car slid into a ditch. She called a local garage they sent a tow truck and she was soon on her way to work at casey school. On her lunch break a few hours later lindsey got stuck again. The same tow truck rescued her. Finally at four o clock she headed home. However before she arrived she went off the road again this time knocking down a mailbox spinning around and ending up in yet another ditch. Down the road came the same tow truck how embarasing. Nonetheless she arrived home safe and sound resolving to learn how to drive better in snow.

Later that night after rodney and lindsey had eaten the phone rang and rodney answered it. It's the tow truck driver deer he called to her. He wants to know if its OK to put the tow truck away!

SPELLING BOX	1. _____	2. _____
3. _____	4. _____	5. _____

13. Review of Punctuation and Capitalization II

Directions: Add capital letters and punctuation marks where they are needed in the story. Circle the five misspelled words. Rewrite them correctly in the Spelling Box.

Tony was a sixteen year old boy and he had just passed his drivers lisence exam. Whenever he got the chance he drove other family members wherever they needed to go.

One day it was a beautiful day in early may tony was driving with his grandpa in his grandpas four wheel drive vehicle down a bumpy dusty dirt road. He didnt know how to control the car very well however he kept on going. A little embarrassed about his poor driving he decided to make an excuse. The sun and shadows on the road make it hard to see the potholes he said lamely.

don't worry my boy grandpa said. you're getting most of them!

Pulling back onto the paved road, tony began driving faster. unfortunately he soon saw flashing blue lights behind him a sure sign that a patrolman had spotted him speeding. Tony pulled off the road and he stopped the car. sorry officer he said its my grandpas car and it doesn't have cruse control.

The trooper stuck his head in the window looking for the dashboard. young man he said gruffly it may not have cruise control but it does have a speedometer. Nonetheless he let tony go with a warning probably dew to the boys youth.

Tony continued home watching the speed limit carefully. Soon he had gotten over his near miss and he decided to munch on an apple. It wasn't until he tossed the core out the window that he realized the same police car was still following him. Once again the policeman in a much sterner mood pulled tony over.

Tony joked nervously that he was just trying to clean up the roadside. The apple core of course could serve as a home for ants which would then clean up tiny bits of liter improving the envirment.

Seeing the big tough trooper cracking a smile tony thought he had it made. Then the trooper said pulling out his ticket book OK lets see your building permit!

SPELLING BOX	1. _____	2. _____
3. _____	4. _____	5. _____

14. Review of Punctuation and Capitalization III

Directions: Add capital letters and punctuation marks where they are needed in each example below. Circle the five misspelled words. Rewrite them correctly in the Spelling Box.

1. Lacey was applying for a secretarial job a position she really wanted. She arrived at the personal office at 10 30 a m on friday june 21. While completing the application she was careful to dot all her i s and cross all her t s. Lacey a recent graduate of w b murrah high school really wanted this job! She came to the question what would you consider your strengths for this position? Lacey thought a minute then answered two of my strengths are spelling and proofreading and on this application the word applicent is misspelled. Lacey got the job!

2. Abbey a student in mrs a b wrights english class had the assignment of writing a five paragraph essay. She chose the following for her topic chivalry is dead. Her teacher returned the paper without Abbeys hoped for *A* s or *B* s. It not only had the grade of *C* but it also had the comment Chivarly is not only dead it is also mispelled.

3. The high school english teacher mr. j w barfield had been explaining the ins and outs of grammar and punctuation for weeks. In fact the months lessons had contained little else much to the students dismay they found it boring.

   Finally the lesson plan switched to poetry a welcome change for the students. One day as the class was reading the works of a modern poet one student seemed puzzled. I don't get it mr barfield he said how come the poet uses no capital letters and misspells some of the words?

   That's called poetic license mr barfield explained.

   Oh the young man replied appearing relieved. How can I apply for one?

SPELLING BOX	1. _____	2. _____
3. _____	4. _____	5. _____

     Find the Errors! II

15. Subject-Verb Agreement

Directions: Underline the correct verb form in each pair of verbs. Circle the five
misspelled words. Write them correctly in the Spelling Box.

Three women, Jena, Yolanda, and Ann, were shipwrecked on a desserted island. Each of
them (was, were) without any supplies or extra clothing. Several coconut trees (was, were) growing nearby to provide shade and food. A small spring, surrounded by mossy rocks, (was, were) a
source of fresh water.

Jena, along with Yolanda, (was, were) the adventurous sort. She decided to explore the
island. Neither (was, were) able to persuade Ann to join them. As far as Jena was concerned,
boredom, as well as the poor selection of food, (was, were) reason enough to explore their environs. Besides, sunbathing, as well as recovering from the ordeal of the wreck, (was, were) getting
to be boring.

Both Jena and Yolanda (was, were) eager to begin. They (was, were) able to circumvent the
perimeter of the island in just under fourty minutes. Neither rocks nor an extremly high tide
(was, were) able to slow them down.

The next of their options (was, were) to climb the hill on the north side of the island. It was
a pleasant climb; both wildflowers and tall grasses (was, were) plentiful. But neither food nor
supplies (was, were) to be found.

Suddenly, Yolanda, the more observant of the two, (was, were) overcome with excitement.
On the ground, nearly hidden in the tall grasses, (was, were) a brass lamp. The lamp, in both
shape and color, (was, were) exactly like the famed Aladdin's lamp. Both Yolanda and Jena (was,
were) in agreement on hurrying back to show Ann the lamp.

Jena rubbed the lamp, and everyone (was, were) surprised when a genie appeared! Each
woman (was, were) granted one wish. Yolanda went first. Her wish (was, were) for a helicopter,
and she flew away, disapearing into the sky. Jena, unlike the others, (was, were) not entirely
afraid of boats, so she wished for a sailboat and sailed away. Ann was lonely, so her wish (was,
were) for her two friends to return.

SPELLING BOX	1. _____	2. _____
3. _____	4. _____	5. _____

16. Principal Parts of Verbs

Directions: Underline the correct form of the verb in each pair below. Circle the five misspelled words. Write them correctly in the Spelling Box.

Mr. Bishop had just (got, gotten) back from a wonderful three-week vacation in Australia. He had (ate, eaten) a lot of fabulous seafood and had (drank, drunk) some of the fine local wines. Each day he had (rise, rose, risen) early and had (ate, eaten) a large breakfast. After this, he had (lay, lain, laid) down for a brief nap. Soon he had (sat, set) out for the day's adventure.

On the way home, Mr. Bishop (sat, set) on the plane for 16 hours. He (lay, laid) the seat back as far as it would go. Nonetheless, he (slept, sleep) very little. He was able to (take, took) full advantage of the personnel servise and fine meals offered.

Needless to say, when Mr. Bishop arrived home, he found that his weight had (rose, risen) about 10 pounds. He was embarassed and sorry he had (set, sit) foot on the scales! But he (goed, went) in to the doctor for advice. The doctor put him on a diet.

"I want you to eat normally for two days, then skip a day," the doctor (told, telled) him sternly. "Repeat this procedure for two weeks. Your weight should have (shrank, shrunk) considerably by then. You should have (lost, losed) five pounds."

When Mr. Bishop (went, gone) back to the doctor two weeks later, he (steps, stepped) on the scales. Sure enough, he had (loose, lost) ten pounds! "Alright!" he exclaimed.

"A noticable improvement! Did you follow my directions?" the doctor asked.

Mr. Bishop nodded. "But it (wasn't, weren't) easy. I (think, thought) I was going to faint on each third day."

"From hunger?" (asks, asked) the doctor.

"No," Mr. Bishop (said, says). "From skipping!"

SPELLING BOX	1. _____	2. _____
3. _____	4. _____	5. _____

17. Consistent Verb Tense

Directions: Decide if the anecdote below should be written in the past or present tense. Then make the changes needed to make the tense consistent and correct throughout. Circle the five misspelled words. Write them correctly in the Spelling Box.

Maggie, a high school student, asks her father, "Dad, can you sign your name with your eyes closed?"

Her dad was perplexed. "I guess so. Why, dear?"

"My report card came in the mail today," she answers.

Maggie's dad is not happy when he sees her grades. Her math grade was a *C*, but she has *D*'s in all her other classes.

They sit down to talk about her study habits. Maggie maintains that she studied at least two hours every night. Maggie's dad decided to observe her study habits the following night. He plans to determine what changes she might make to improve her efficiency and acheive better grades.

Maggie's study time was from 7 to 9 P.M., and she follows this scedule carefully. Here is how she uses her time that night:

For 15 minutes she looks for the peice of paper on which she had wrote her assignments. It takes 17 minutes for her to call a friend to get the assignment plus the latest news. Two trips to the bathroom adds up to 10 more minutes. It was important to keep up her strength, so Maggie spends 12 minutes concocting a snack in the kitchen. Maggie checks the TV schedule in the newspaper. She decided what she would watch after she finishes her homework. This takes another 6 minutes.

Maggie is getting frustrated. She spent 15 minutes complaning that the teacher does not explain the assignment. Another 20 minutes elapsed as Maggie complains about the teacher. Maggie says she is mean and did not understand kids.

Maggie finally sits down at her desk and looked at her book. She thumbs through a stack of paper for 15 minutes. For the final 10 minutes of the study period, Maggie trys to get her dad to do the work for her. At 9 P.M. sharp, Maggie closes her books, turned on the TV and said, "You've got to admitt, Dad, I worked pretty hard tonight!"

SPELLING BOX	1. _____	2. _____
3. _____	4. _____	5. _____

18. Case of Personal Pronouns

Directions: Underline the correct personal pronoun from each pair in parentheses. Circle the five misspelled words. Write them correctly in the Spelling Box.

1. Boss: "How come (you and Bill, Bill and yourself) are only carrying one sack when the other men are carrying two?"

    Worker: "I suppose (its, it's) because (they are, their) too lazy to make two trips the way (Bill and me, Bill and I) do."

2. Boss: "I'd like to go through one whole day without scolding (you and he, you and him)."

    Worker: "Well, you certainly have (my, mine) consent."

3. Worker #1: "I told (our, our's) boss that (you and me, you and I) are perfect."

    Worker #2: "Did (she, her) agree with you?"

    Worker #1: "I don't know. She (haven't, hasn't) stopped laughing at (I, me) yet!"

4. For years, Mr. Allen's secretery was fifteen minutes late to work every day. Then one morning (she, her) was only ten minutes late. Mr. Allen remarked, "(You, Your) being late bothers me. But this is the earliest you've ever been late to this job of (yours, your's).

5. Worker: My boss was a very tactful man; a master of tact was (he, him). He called me in one day and said, "When the vice president and (me, I) think about it, (we, I) don't know how (we're, were) going to get along without you, but starting Monday, (we're, were) going to try!"

6. Phil and Art were in the stockroom of a large warehouse loungeing against a packing crate when the boss came in. Addressing Phil, who was wearing a name tag, the boss asked, "(You, Your) standing around makes me furius! How much are (you and he, you and him) getting a week?"

    "About $200 a week each," came (they're, their) answer.

    "Here's (your, you're) $200 apiece. Now get out of here and don't come back," the boss said angerily.

    Phil and (he, him) put the money in (they're, their) pockets and hurried out.
    The boss saw the stockroom manager and called to (he, him), "How long (has, have) (Phil and him, Phil and he) been working here?"

    "They don't work here. (Phil and him, Phil and he) just delivered a packige!"

SPELLING BOX	1. _____	2. _____
3. _____	4. _____	5. _____

19. Pronoun-Antecedent Agreement

Directions: Correct any errors in pronoun-antecedent or pronoun-verb agreement in the story below by crossing out incorrect words and writing correct ones above them. Circle the five misspelled words. Write them correctly in the Spelling Box.

Ahmed and his friend Jabbar were from the big city, where you don't see much green space. They worked hard to plan his camping trip in the wilds of northern Minnesota. It was the first time either of them had been camping. They were going to a remote spot where you could catch lots of fish. They had hired a fishing guide with an excelent reputation you could rely on.

He and Jabbar found the long trip tired you out. First they took an airplane journey (another first for him) to St. Paul. Then came a 200-mile car trip north. Him and Jabbar made the last leg of his journey by boat. Both was glad it was a motorboat, not a canoe.

When the two got to the guide's cabin, he went inside. The guide stayed outside to finish some of the chores you have to do. Both was surprised to see the pot-bellied stove in a most unusual position, set up on posts nearly three feet off the cabin floor. Neither of the men knew the reasons for her unusual placement.

Jabbar said, "I'm sure it's for a practicle reason. The heat from the stove would dry out green or wet wood placed under them."

"I imagine," said Ahmed, "that the heat from the stove circulates much quicker around the room, thus warming it quicker for you and I."

"Actually," Jabbar replied, warming to his subject, "us both know that warm air rises in a room. Cool air can come in an open window at night so you will not get too hot."

The two men thought hard to get his dilemna figured out. When the guide returned, they asked him to settle the arguement for they.

"It's simple," he explained to he and Ahmed. "When I brought the stove upriver on my boat, I lost one section of stovepipe overbored. So I set the stove up high so you could get the smoke to go out the hole in the roof!"

SPELLING BOX	1. _____	2. _____
3. _____	4. _____	5. _____

20. Clear Pronoun Reference

Directions: Rewrite each of the following sentences, making sure that all pronoun references are clearly stated. Circle the five misspelled words. Write them correctly in the Spelling Box.

1. The teacher told the student that all students were expected to be at school by 8:00 A.M. The student replyed that she understood, but she should go ahead without her if she wasn't there by then!

2. When one student reminded another that he would have a half day of school that morning, he was happy. Then he realised that he would have the other half day that afternoon!

3. A lecturer announced to his audience that the world would end in approximatly nine billion years, and it scared one person badly. He thought he said nine *million* years.

4. When an envelope was crossed with a homing pigeon, it came back every time it was mailed.

5. In Utah there's a lake that's so clear you can look into it and see them making tea in China.

6. He was the new boss at the cheese factory, and this was evident in the sign on his desk, which read "The Big Cheese."

7. Mark worked as a proffessional comedien, which gave him a job that you laugh at.

SPELLING BOX		
	1. _____	2. _____
3. _____	4. _____	5. _____

21. Review of Subject-Verb Agreement and Pronouns

Directions: Underline the correct word in each pair. Circle the five misspelled words. Rewrite them correctly in the Spelling Box.

Julio and Beth both (has, have) landed new jobs in another city. They (are, is) excited about the move, but first they, like most people in this position, (has, have) to sell their house. The two (cleans, clean) each room until (you, they) can't do any more. Finally, everything (is, are) as purfect as (you, they) can make it.

Beth lists (their, they're) house with a real estate agent, and for a few weeks the agent works hard for Julio and (her, she). Julio and Beth (become, becomes) obsessive housekeepers. Every dish (has, have) to be washed imediately. Each piece of clothing (has, have) to be hung up or put away. The carpets (is, are) vacumed daily. Every particle of dust (is, are) removed. Every room (has, have) to be perfect at all times. After all, no one (is, are) sure when a prospective buyer might show up at (their, they're) door.

Then one day, the doorbell (ring, rings) without warning at 8 A.M. Julio, as well as Beth, (open, opens) the door. There they see (their, they're) real estate agent with a couple from Alaska who (want, wants) to see the house. The agent (doesn't, don't) make much of an apology. He says that there had been no time to call. The Alaskans (has, have) to catch a plain in an hour.

So, three people (make, makes) (their, they're) way through the kitchen which (is, are) dirty and full of dishes. Next stop: the bedroom with (its, it's) unmade beds! Several towels (is, are) strewn across the bathroom floor. Beth, as well as Julio, (is, are) still in a bathrobe. In addition, Beth (is, are) sporting curlers in her hair. The whole picture (doesn't, don't) at all give the image the couple (hope, hopes) to present. They don't remember (ever, never) being so embarrassed!

The next day, the real estate agent (phone, phones) Julio to say that the couple from Alaska (has, have) bought the house! He then told Beth and (he, him) what the buyer had said about the house: "That house, of all the ones we looked at, (has, have) a warm, lived-in look, just like ours!"

SPELLING BOX	1. _____	2. _____
3. _____	4. _____	5. _____

22. Dangling or Misplaced Modifiers

Directions: Rewrite each sentence below that contains a dangling or misplaced modifier. If the sentence is correct as written, write CORRECT. Circle the five misspelled words. Write them correctly in the Spelling Box.

1. The bride was given away by her father wearing her mother's wedding viel.

2. Falling from a tree, the amature photographer captured some beautiful autumn leaves.

3. Writing all night long, the term paper was finally complete.

4. The repairman arrived to fix the air conditioner with the helpful smile.

5. The bird-watcher saw the two birds fighting with his binoculers.

6. After taking a shower, the bed looked inviting.

7. Nailed to a telephone pole, I saw one of his campane signs.

8. The sign at the movies read: "No children admited without an adult under eight years of age."

9. The plane took off on time after a rushed breakfast.

SPELLING BOX	1. _____	2. _____
3. _____	4. _____	5. _____

23. Sentence Fragments and Run-on Sentences

Directions: Rewrite the story below correcting all sentence fragments and run-on sentences. (There will be more than one correct way to do this.) Circle the five misspelled words. Write them correctly in the Spelling Box.

A couple was driving through a deserted area of Wyoming. Flat ground. A straight road. Not another car in sight for miles. The weather was perfect clear blue skys. Not a cloud in sight.

The couple began to drive faster and faster. A policeman sudenly out of nowhere. Pulled them over, blue lights flashing.

"I'm going to have to give you a ticket," the policeman sternly. "Driving at one hunderd miles per hour not acceptable."

"That can't be acurate! Only been driving ten minutes," the man said.

Noticing the couple was wearing seat belts. The trooper began to put his ticket book away he was going to let them off with a warning.

Then man (unwisely) added. "Officer, when you drive the speeds I do. You've got to wear a safety belt."

SPELLING BOX	1. _____	2. _____
3. _____	4. _____	5. _____

24. Varying Sentence Styles

Directions: The story below is written in short, choppy sentences with no variety of length or style. Rewrite the story using a variety of sentence patterns. You may combine sentences to form compound or complex sentences. Circle the five misspelled words. Rewrite them correctly in the Spelling Box.

I was driving with my younger brother. He had just gotten his learners permit. It was the first time he had driven the car since getting his permit.

At first, I was pleased. He was handling the busy road well. We past a traffic light. The lanes shifted. He was stradling the dotted line. The line was dividing two lanes of traffic. "Get in your own lane," I yelled.

He looked at me. He was puzzled. "Which one is mine?" he asked.

This crisis was over. We came to a traffic light. It was yellow. It was about to turn red. My brother stopped the car. He did this in a hurry. The tires squealed.

By now he was a bit shaken. He sat at the light. He was catching his breathe and looking around. He did not notise when the light changed to green. Then it turned yellow, red, green, yellow, and back to red.

At this point, a policeman walked up. He walked up to the car. He taped on the window. "That's all the colors we've got around here, boys," he said.

SPELLING BOX	1. _____	2. _____
3. _____	4. _____	5. _____

25. Using Interesting Language

Directions: Rewrite the story below, replacing tired adjectives, verbs, and nouns with more specific, interesting words. Replace trite expressions or clichés with more interesting language. Circle the five misspelled words. Rewrite them correctly in the Spelling Box.

It was a nice day. The weather was good. It was a nice temperture, and it was not raining. The whether was pretty as a picture. It was a great day to be outside.

A young boy was playing outside. He went down a path to a creek. He skipped stones across the water. He rolled up his pants and waded in.

He liked exploring along the banks of the creak. Seeing some movement in the grass, he looked down. There he found a frog.

The frog looked at him and said, "Kiss me and I will turn into a pretty princess!"

The boy looked carefuly at the frog. Then quitely as a mouse he put the frog in his pocket and kept on looking around.

The frog said, "Hey, why didn't you kiss me?"

"Silly frog," the boy said. "I'd rather have a talking frog than a princess any day!"

SPELLING BOX	1. _____	2. _____
3. _____	4. _____	5. _____

26. Avoiding Wordiness

Directions: Rewrite each sentence, eliminating wordiness. (You will not rewrite the last paragraph, which is the reporter's story.) Circle the five misspelled words. Rewrite them correctly in the Spelling Box.

The young 20-year-old reporter had just started his first begining job as a cub reporter for a major big newspaper in Dallas, Texas, a city in Texas.

The young reporter was hardworking and accurite; he worked hard and got the details right. His news stories were interesting and well-written.

But there was one and only one problem. His stories were always much too lengthy and long for the space the newspaper could allot and allow for them because they had to be a certain length to fit in the space.

His editor talked to him several times with no affect. On this day, the editor called him in once again and said, "You don't never listen to me. I see I must repeat myself again. I think your stories are too long, in my opinion. You must keep your copy short and to the point. For your next story, please include only the bear facts. Eventualy in the long run you'll get it."

Later that day, the reporter was reassigned again to report on a train accident. He turned in this copy:

> "B. Sampson walked out onto the subway tracks to see if the train was coming. It was. Age 42."

SPELLING BOX

1. _____   2. _____

3. _____   4. _____   5. _____

---

27. Making Comparisons Correctly

Directions: Underline the correct word in each pair of words in parentheses. Circle the five misspelled words. Write them correctly in the Spelling Box.

A woman had inspected the merchandice in every department in the (largest, most largest) department store in town. She liked to dress (good, well). She knew she looked (good, well) in blue, but she couldn't decide which was (more, most) attractive of two blue blouses. She needed slacks (bad, badly), so she looked at many pairs, but she couldn't choose which was (better, best). Shoes were on sale; she looked at pair after pair declaring each one (uglier, ugliest) than the last. She found a coat she liked better than (any, any other) coat. The store didn't have the (most prettiest, prettiest) coat in her size. That was the (more, most) disapointing of all!

She moved on to the cosmetics department. The scent of the cologne was (most, more) overpowering than (the perfume, the perfume's). This store carried more brands than (anyone, anyone else). The light floral scents were the (most, more) appealing of all the scents. But the woman couldn't decide if she liked the lily or peach scent (better, best). Both smelled (good, well). She felt (bad, badly) about not choosing anything to buy.

The woman continued to the housewares department. Of all the departments in the store this was her (favorite, most favorite) because this store had the (better, best) selection in town. The prices were (less, least) expensive than the other (store, stores'). She picked up and examined (more, most) of the items in the linens department.

Then she browsed in the china section. Two china patterns looked (good, well), but she couldn't chose which would go (better, best) in her home. The crystal was the (less, least) economical choice of all the items in that department.

So she continued throughout the store. By the end of the day she had handled more items than (any, any other) customer in the histery of the store. Finally, a manager aproached her. "Ma'am, I feel (bad, badly) for asking, but are you shopping here?"

"Certainly," she replied in a surprised tone. "What else would I be doing?"

"Well, ma'am," he replied. "I thought perhaps you were doing an inventory."

SPELLING BOX	1. _____	2. _____
3. _____	4. _____	5. _____

28. Correct Usage

Directions: Underline the correct word in each pair of words in parentheses. Circle the five misspelled words. Write them correctly in the Spelling Box.

Caroline had been working at the same office job for quite (a while, awhile). The job was (alot, a lot) of work, and there were (fewer, less) benifits every year (accept, except) a fairly reasonable pay raise. (Irregardless, Regardless), Caroline (couldn't hardly, could hardly) stand to go to work every day. It was an (all together, altogether) unsatisfactery situation. She could see little choice (besides, beside) looking for a new job.

Caroline decided to (proceed, precede) with her job search. She hoped she could find something different (from, than) what she (all ready, already) had. Caroline wrote her resume on her computor. She listed her (past, passed) experience. She wrote a cover letter that she hopped would have a positive (affect, effect) on prospective employors. She proofread the letter (good, well). Then she signed it "(Respectively, Respectfully) yours."

Caroline e-mailed her letter to dozens of potential employers. She attached her resume to each one. Since the job market was good, she hoped she would get several good offers (among, between) which she could choose. But she had far (fewer, less) offers than she expected; in fact, after two weeks had (passed, past) she had none at all! She couldn't imagine what could (of, have) gone wrong. She certainly didn't want to (emigrate, immigrate) to another country to find a job!

Finally, she received a message from one of the prospective employers. (That there, That) message explained why her efforts hadn't gone (further, farther) toward landing her a job.

The message (said, says), "Your resume was not attached to your letter as stated. However, I was pleased to (accept, except) your delicious recipe for chocolate fudge cake!"

SPELLING BOX	1. _____	2. _____
3. _____	4. _____	5. _____

29. Review I

Directions: Rewrite each sentence below, making all corrections necessary. Circle the five misspelled words. Write them correctly in the Spelling Box.

1. Try to always avoid splitting an infinitive.

2. Don't use more words than necessary; don't be wordy; don't be redundant; too many words are superflous and extraneus and unecessary.

3. Use of too many foriegn words is not de rigueur or apropos.

4. Use more or less specific nouns and verbs to make your writing more interesting.

5. Don't never use no double negatives.

6. Writing well, dangling and misplaced modifiers are to be avoided.

7. Verbs and their subjects always has to agree.

8. Proofread your writing carefully to find careless errers and to see if you words out.

9. Good writers do not shift your point of view.

10. This usage rule, unlike many others, are never to be broken.

SPELLING BOX	1. _____	2. _____
3. _____	4. _____	5. _____

30. Review II

Directions: Rewrite each sentence below, making all corrections necessary. Circle the five correctly used, but misspelled words. Write them correctly in the Spelling Box.

A teacher was reveiwing with her class again that weeks vocabulery words. She said In my opinion I think that each of you need to study their words more. On last weeks test you got less corect then I would like to see. So lets go threw the words.

Mike use the word income in a sentence she began.

I open the door and income the dog Mike replied.

Gio try the word information she continued bravely.

Gio said The fighter jets flew information.

The teacher sighed but went on. Miko, please use the word gruesome correctly.

Thats easy Miko replied. I was pretty short last year but this summer I gruesome.

Biswa try the word adverb please.

An adverb is a verb that likes to do math he answered.

No no no shouted the teacher. Lets try the easyest one. Jane the word is décor.

No problum said Jane. D'core is whats in the middle of d'apple!

SPELLING BOX	1. _____	2. _____
3. _____	4. _____	5. _____

31. Review III

Directions: Add corrections where they are needed in the story. Cross out any words that need to be omitted. Add words needed to correct sentence fragments. Circle the five misspelled words. Write them correctly in the Spelling Box.

Norm came home after his first day of school. His father met him at the door and his father asked How did you like going back to school today? his dad said.

Norm said Oh going was all right and coming home was fine too. It was the inbetween part I didn't like. Dad will you please help me with my homework? I have something for every subject. For science I have to write a paragraph about nitrates it must be turned in tomorrow.

Well that's easy son. When you call long distence their cheaper than day rates! Dad replied.

I also have to look up about the law of gravity it keeps us from falling of the earth, Norm said.

That should be interesting. But I forget, what kept us from falling off before the law was past? Dad answered.

I don't know, said Norm. Now I also have to write an autobiography for English it should be one page long. Due next Tuesday.

An autobiography is a cars life story look one up on the Internet dad said.

I also need to prepare some information on weather or not television will take the place of newspapers.

Of course it wont! said Dad indignantly. Did you ever try to kill a fly with a rolled up television?

For History I need to know something about the Iron Age Norm continued.

His dad replied "that he was sorry but he was a bit rusty on that one."

To top it all off, in math I have to find the common denominator. Norm said.

Well my boy they must have really lost it they were looking for it back when I was in school. Dad said.

SPELLING BOX	1. _____	2. _____
3. _____	4. _____	5. _____

32. Review IV

Directions: Make corrections where they are needed in the story. Add words to correct sentence fragments. Circle the misspelled words. Rewrite them correctly in the Spelling Box.

Gary a sophmore at belhaven college was planning to fly home for Thanksgiving break. Since the day before Thanksgiving is one of the busiest flying days of the year he was buying his tickets a month in advance it was a harder job than he thought there were a lot of choices to make.

He had the choice of calling a travel agent calling the airlines directly or using the Internet to search for fares. Easier to use the Internet to compare fares. First of all he had to chose which days to leave and return it made a big difference in the fair. Tuesdays, Wednesdays and Saturdays the cheapest days to fly. Sundays the most expensive.

Next he had to choose the time of day. The 8:00 am and 5:00 pm flights were more money, that was probably because these flights was more popular with business travilers.

He also had to choose if he wanted a direct flight the ones with stops were a little less money that was important since he was on a tight budget.

Sitting at his dell computer his eyes became tired. Nonetheless he kept on entering choices trying to come up with the best deal. Finding a ticket for $99 the purchase was made he put it on his mastercard.

Arriving at jones international airport on the day of the flight Gary had the choice of the close in parking lot at $15 per day or the cheap lot with the shuttle bus for $7 a day he chose the latter. He rushed to the delta airlines ticket counter where he had to choose a window isle or middle seat.

Settling into his narrow seat the stewardess approached shortly after takeoff. She asked Would you like to have a meal?

What are my choices he replied.

Yes or no.

SPELLING BOX	1. _____	2. _____
3. _____	4. _____	5. _____

33. Review V

Directions: Make corrections where they are needed in the story. Circle the five misspelled words. Rewrite them correctly in the Spelling Box.

It was a beautiful Spring morning and the sun was shining and the sky was blue. Several wispy white clouds was floating lazily in the air. The dafodils as well as a tulip was poking its head out of the ground. The grass was getting green and many of the trees was begining to leaf out. Each of the birds in the yard were singing their finest song. It was all together a very fine morning.

The previous week had been Spring Break. All of the students was granted an entire week off from school. The weather had cooperated and everyone had enjoyed being outside in your yard or out at the lake.

But now it was Monday morning and time to go back to school. The return to classes books homework. Something no one looked forward to. But now the dreaded day had arrived. It was Monday morning.

A mother walked into her son's room. She said Time to get up and go to school!

But I don't want to said the son. Pulling his pillow over his head the bed became still again.

Once again the mother came into the room. All were dark and still. Looking at the bed a big lump in the middle could still be seen.

You must get up the mother insisted you'll be late.

But everyone hate me replied the son. Not one person in that entire school like me neither the teachers nor the students likes me. They all try to avoid me when they see me coming they turn and go the other way. Not only that the food in the cafeteria is lousy.

The mom listened to all this as long as she could stand it. Be that as it may she said finally you have no choice you have to go your 35 years old and you're the principle.

SPELLING BOX	1. _____	2. _____
3. _____	4. _____	5. _____

Find the Errors! II

34. Review VI

Directions: Rewrite each sentence below, making all corrections necessary. Circle the five misspelled words. Rewrite them correctly in the Spelling Box.

A city man was driving down a country road about 50 miles from salt lake city utah. It was a beautiful area near the wasatch mountains. He had read about this seenic drive in the best selling book round the mountain by sheila b. cumming and looking forward to it for a long time.

Suddenly his car sputtered to a stop near a field where a heard of cows were grazing. He looked at his instrument panel niether the gas nor the oil were low. He got out the official owners manual it was entitled Keeping Your Car Running by ira fuse. Finding nothing helpful in the book, the tires were checked.

The man opened the hood and peered in at the engine nothing seemed wrong. Then he noticed a cow from the large herd were watching him.

I do believe it's your radiater said the cow.

The man was surprised he ran to the nearest farmhouse. Knocked on the door. Opened by an old farmer. One of your cows just give me advise about my car the man shouted to the farmer.

The farmer leaned against the door. The spotted cow with the two big brown spots on her side the others are solid colored but just that one is spotted the farmer asked questioningly.

Yes yes that's the one the man excitedly replied in great excitement.

Oh that's Ethel said the farmer. Don't pay attention to her she don't know nothing about cars.

SPELLING BOX	1. _____	2. _____
3. _____	4. _____	5. _____

35. Review VII

Directions: Add corrections where they are needed in the story. Cross out words as needed to avoid wordiness. Circle the five misspelled words. Rewrite them correctly in the Spelling Box.

It had been a long hot dry summer in the rocky mountains of the Western United States. Wildfires were braking out daily across the region. Some were ignited by careless campers others by lightning striking tall lodgepole pines. The fire that was later named the willie fire caused by a lighted cigerette thrown out the window of a car traveling down the cooke city highway. The fire spread quick. Soon threatening to overrun the small town of red lodge a small town that was not very large nestled in a mountain vally.

Major newspapers magazines and television networks rushed reporters and photographers to the scene quickly. They sent them as fast as possible. Each of these media were billing the willie fire as your top news story of the week.

When the first photographer arrived in red lodge. He saw that the smoke was so thick. He could not shoot pictures of the firefighters from the ground. There was too much smoke. However he was able to hire a plane.

It was a short drive to the grassy field. That served as the town's airport. He saw a small cessna plane warming up and he ran and jumped in. He told the pilot to take off. Within a few minutes they were airborne in the air.

The photographer asked the pilot to turn West and make low circling passes to circle over the area where the firefighters was fighting the fire. He like all good photographers were hoping to get some good action shots of the firefighters in action.

Why asked the pilot.

Because I'm a photographer. Needing to take pictures. I have my kodak film loaded and my nikon camera ready for action.

The pilot looked stunned he was speechless and couldn't speak for a minute. Finally after a while he stamered you mean your not my flight instructor?

SPELLING BOX	1. _____	2. _____
3. _____	4. _____	5. _____

Find the Errors! II Posttest

Directions: Each sentence below has one or more errors. In the space below each
sentence, rewrite the sentence correcting all errors. Circle the 10 misspelled
words in the Posttest and spell them correctly when you rewrite the
sentences. (Missing capital letters do not count as misspellings.)

1. The algebra II class of forest hill high school a well known maryland school visited the
   u s mint in philadelphia pennsylvania.

2. Their are many spanish speaking americans in the miami area so many signs are
   printed in both english and spanish (for example: stop! and para!).

3. Our new street address is unusual it is 333 33rd street (a lot of 3s).

4. Hanging on a peg I saw my brothers new blue jacket which he had lost last Wenesday.

5. The fifteen year old girl as well as her two brothers go to washington high school and
   they are hardly never on time to school in the morning.

6. The runing back carried the football fifty yards slides across the goal line and scored
   the wining touchdown.

7. When the little girl lost site of her mother in the store, she was scared.

(continued)

Find the Errors! II Posttest (continued)

8. William and Lydia are getting married. On the honeymoon traveling to the beach. Which they both love.

9. Luis and Marta are on the cross country team, they both like to run sprints.

10. Eudora Welty was a writer. She was born in Jackson, Mississippi. She wrote novels. She wrote short stories. She was famous.

11. In my opinion I think that I need to redo that job again.

12. Thomas Edison was one of the worlds most best inventers; the lightbulb was one of his more usefuler inventions.

13. The dog has all ready eaten it's dinner and is laying on the floor under the busted table.

14. My science paper which I titled affects of light on plant growth did good in the science fair and every one liked it.

15. In his book tales from margaritaville jimmy buffet said It takes no more time to see the good side of life than to see the bad.

Teacher's Guide

Background Information

Capital Letters
Student Exercises 1 and 2

These exercises deal with the proper use of capitalization, according to the following rules:

1. Capitalize all proper nouns. A proper noun names a particular person, place, or thing. (Common nouns name one of a group of persons, places, or things and are not capitalized.) The following proper nouns should be capitalized:

    a. Names of people and initials of people's names. (*Examples:* Jake R. Lobb, J.R.L.)

    b. Titles used in front of a person's name. (*Examples:* Dr. Ross, Senator French)

    c. A title when it is used in direct address. (*Examples:* What time can we meet, Governor? The governor did not have time to meet with us.)

    d. Names of places, such as countries, cities, mountains, streets, and oceans. (*Examples:* Argentina, New York, the Rocky Mountains, First Street, Atlantic Ocean)

    e. Names of stars and planets, except *sun* and *moon.* The word *Earth* used as the name of our planet, unless it is preceded by the word *the.*

    f. Nationalities, peoples, and languages. (*Examples:* Irish, Mayan, Latin)

    g. Days, months, holidays, and special events. (*Examples:* Tuesday, May, Christmas, the Crawfish Festival)

    h. Names of historical events and periods, documents, and awards. (*Examples:* the Constitution, the Revolutionary War, the Pulitzer Prize)

    i. Names of businesses, government agencies, political parties, clubs, and schools. (*Examples:* Ford Motor Company, the Defense Department, a Democrat, the Boy Scouts, Georgia Tech)

    j. Brand names of products. (*Examples:* Coca-Cola, Tide detergent)

    k. Names of trains, ships, planes, and spacecraft. (*Examples:* Amtrak, the U.S.S. *Constitution,* the *Concorde, Challenger*)

    l. Names of monuments, bridges, buildings, etc. (*Examples:* the Lincoln Monument, Brooklyn Bridge, Empire State Building)

    m. The words *Mother, Father, Grandma,* etc., if they are used as a person's name. Do not capitalize them if they are used in such phrases as "my mother."

    n. Direction words if they indicate a part of the country. Do not capitalize them if they merely indicate a direction. (*Examples:* They live in the West. Drive two blocks west.)

    o. Capitalize references to religions, denominations, sacred works , books of the Bible, deities, or prophets. Do not capitalize *god* or *goddess* when it refers to gods of mythology. (*Examples:* God, the Bible, the book of John, the goddess Athena)

    p. Abbreviations of proper nouns. (*Example:* N. Congress Ave.)

    q. The first word and all important words in titles of books, plays, articles, paintings, periodicals, movies, musical compositions, poems, and other works of art. Capitalize small words like *a, an, the, in, on,* etc., only if they begin or end the title. (*Example:* I am reading the book *The Old Man and the Sea.*)

r. Common nouns used as part of a proper noun. For example, in the proper noun *Morrison Elementary School,* the word *school* is capitalized because it is part of the proper noun.

s. Do not capitalize prepositions, the word *and,* or the articles *a, an,* or *the* when used as part of a proper noun. (*Example:* the Statue of Liberty)

2. Capitalize most proper adjectives. (*Examples:* Irish lace, English setter, Chinese writings)

3. Capitalize the first word of a direct quotation that is a complete sentence. (*Example:* She said, "Come with me.") If the quoted sentence is interrupted by a phrase such as *he said,* do not capitalize the second part of the quotation. (*Example:* "Come with me," she said, "to try that new restaurant.")

4. Capitalize the first word of a sentence.

5. Capitalize the word *I* and its contractions.

6. Capitalize the name of a school subject if it comes from the name of a country. Capitalize the name of a course followed by a Roman numeral. Do not capitalize other subjects. (*Examples:* English, French, Spanish, Chemistry II, chemistry, biology)

7. Capitalize the first word of each line of a poem (unless the original poem did not do so).

8. Capitalize abbreviations formed from initial letters. (*Examples:* the NAACP, AIDS)

9. Capitalize abbreviations related to dates and times. (*Examples:* A.M., B.C.)

10. Capitalize state abbreviations. (*Example:* MT)

Commas
Student Exercises 3 and 4

Use commas to:

1. Separate parts of an address.
   (*Example:* They have lived at 4315 Hill Street, Quincy, Illinois, since 1987.)

2. Separate parts of a date.
   (*Example:* It happened on Monday, October 18, 2002, at 10 A.M.)

3. Set off a noun in direct address.
   (*Example:* Class, read Chapter Two for tomorrow.)

4. Set off appositives (pairs of adjacent nouns that play the same grammatical role in a sentence).
   (*Example:* Our neighbor, Charles Wilson, is a doctor.)

5. Separate three or more items in a series.
   (*Example:* I ordered a hamburger, fries, and a soft drink.)

6. Separate a quotation from the rest of the sentence.
   (*Example:* "I'll help," volunteered Miguel, "if you need me to.")

7. Separate two or more adjectives preceding a noun.
   (*Example:* I settled into my cozy, soft, new armchair.)

8. Separate two or more independent clauses joined by *and, or, but, nor, for,* or *yet.*
   (*Example:* We went to school early, and we talked to all our friends.)

9. Set off nonessential clauses and nonessential participial phrases.
   (*Examples:* My neighbor, who loves animals, works for the Animal Rescue League.

   The boy, running down the stairs, tripped and fell.)

Use commas:

10. After an introductory word like *yes, no, well,* or *oh.*
    (*Example:* Yes, I'd like to see that movie.)

11. After an introductory participial phrase.
    (*Example:* Frightened by the noise, the child started to cry.)

12. After a series of introductory prepositional phrases.
    (*Example:* Near the tree by the edge of the water, we sat and talked.)

13. After a long introductory prepositional phrase.

    (*Example:* Up the dark, winding, steep circular staircase, the women walked carefully.)

14. After an introductory adverb clause.

    (*Example:* After the organist finished playing, the audience clapped.)

15. After the salutation of a friendly letter.

    (*Example:* Dear Susan,)

16. After the closing of any letter.

    (*Example:* Sincerely yours,)

17. After a name followed by *Jr., Sr.,* or *M.D.*

    (*Example:* My father is John Edwards, Jr., and he is a lawyer.)

Use commas to:

18. Set off parenthetical expressions.

    (*Example:* She won, not surprisingly, first place in each event.)

19. Set off parts of a reference that direct the reader to the exact source.

    (*Example:* The assignment was to read the *Odyssey,* Book 10, pages 5–6.)

20. Set off a tag question.

    (*Example:* You'll deposit this money, won't you?)

Avoid using any unnecessary commas!

Quotation Marks
Student Exercise 5

1. Use quotation marks before and after a direct quotation.

   (*Example:* Joan said, "I will walk the dog after supper.")

2. Do not use quotation marks for an indirect quotation.

   (*Example:* Joan said that she would walk the dog after supper.)

3. When writing a dialogue or conversation, begin a new paragraph and use new quotation marks for each change of speaker.

   (*Examples:* "What would you like to do tonight?" asked Joel.

   "Well, there is a new movie in town," answered Selena, "but it might not be one that would appeal to you."

   "What is it?" asked Joel.)

4. Use quotation marks around titles of short stories, one-act plays, articles, songs, poems, and themes.

   (*Examples:* I read "The Telltale Heart" by Edgar Allan Poe.

   I memorized "The Road Not Taken" by Robert Frost.)

5. Use single quotation marks to enclose a quotation within a quotation.

   (*Example:* The fire marshall told us, "It is against the law to yell 'Fire!' in a crowded room if there is not really a fire.")

6. Use quotation marks around unusual expressions or slang.

   (*Example:* My brother's team yells "You da man" to cheer a job well done.)

7. Always put a comma or period inside the closing quotation marks.

   (*Example:* Sali said, "I am taking Spanish this year.")

8. Always put a semicolon or colon outside closing quotation marks.

   (*Example:* My dad said, "We can't afford it"; my mother said, "Maybe next year.")

9. Place a question mark or exclamation point inside the closing quotation marks when it is part of the quotation.

   (*Example:* I said, "When will you be ready to go?")

10. Place a question mark or exclamation point outside the closing quotation marks when it is a part of the whole sentence.

    (*Example:* When will you ever say the words, "I'm ready to go"?)

Hyphens, Colons, and Semicolons
Student Exercise 6

1. Use a **hyphen** to divide a word between syllables at the end of a line.

2. Use a hyphen with compound numbers from twenty-one to ninety-nine.

   (*Example:* She will turn twenty-one on her birthday.)

3. Use a hyphen with fractions used as adjectives.

   (*Example:* The sale price is a one-third reduction.)

4. Use a hyphen with prefixes such as *self-, ex-, all-*.

   (*Example:* He is a self-made man.)

5. Use hyphens when using a compound adjective in front of a noun.

   (*Example:* He is a well-liked student.)

6. Use a hyphen to show a span of numbers.

   (*Example:* The teacher assigned pages 50–60.)

7. Use a **colon** when you write the time in numerals.

   (*Example:* The time is 10:30 P.M.)

8. Use a colon before a list of items, especially after expressions such as *as follows*.

   (*Example:* The plan for the day is as follows: eat, swim, nap, eat, swim, nap.)

9. Do not use a colon to introduce a list if the list follows a preposition or a verb.

   (*Example:* To make banana bread you need to have flour, bananas, and salt.)

10. Use a colon between chapter and verse of a Bible citation.

    (*Example:* Today's lesson is from John 3:16.)

11. Use a colon after the salutation of a business letter.

    (*Example:* Dear Sirs:)

12. Use a colon before a long, formal, or definitive statement or quotation.

    (*Example:* On the subject of raising taxes, the president had this to say: "Read my lips—no new taxes.")

13. When quoting more than one line of poetry or more than four lines of prose, use a colon after the introductory statement.

    (*Example:* In his poem "The Road Not Taken," Robert Frost states:)

14. Use a **semicolon** to separate main clauses not joined by *and, but, or, nor, yet,* or *for* (coordinating conjunctions).

    (*Example:* He loved to play soccer; he was an excellent swimmer as well.)

15. Use a semicolon to separate main clauses that are joined by a conjunctive adverb (such as *however, furthermore, moreover, nevertheless, therefore*).

    (*Example:* I love to swim; however, the water is pretty cold.)

16. Use a semicolon to separate items in a series if the series contains commas.

    (*Example:* Some of my favorite nursery rhymes are "Hickory, Dickory, Dock"; "One, Two, Buckle My Shoe"; and "Mary, Mary, Quite Contrary.")

Apostrophes
Student Exercise 7

1. Use apostrophes to show ownership.

   (*Examples:* Mary's car, the boys' car, the children's toys, my mother-in-law's voice)

2. Use apostrophes to form contractions.

   (*Examples:* I'll, it's)

3. Use an apostrophe and an *s* to form the plurals of figures, symbols, letters, and words referred to as such.

   (*Examples:* There are two *4*'s in my phone number.

   There are 3 *a*'s in the word *banana*.

   Your paragraph has too many *I*'s beginning sentences.)

4. Use an apostrophe in place of omitted numbers in a year.

   (*Example:* I visited Chicago in '02.)

Parentheses
Student Exercise 8

1. Use parentheses to set off supplemental material.

   [*Example*: There is a school uniform (white shirt and blue pants) for grades 1–6.]

2. Do not use a capital letter and period if a complete sentence is put in parentheses within another sentence.

   [*Example*: School uniforms (they are popular with parents) make buying school clothes easier.]

3. Use a capital letter if a complete sentence in parentheses stands on its own.

   [*Example*: School uniforms make buying school clothes easier. (For that reason, they are popular with parents.)]

4. Put a comma, semicolon, or colon after the closing parentheses.

   [*Example*: The room was decorated in school colors (blue and white), and it looked great!]

5. Put a question mark or exclamation point inside the parentheses if it is part of the parenthetical expression.

   [*Example*: He ran the mile in four minutes (Whew!).]

6. Put a question mark or exclamation point outside the parentheses if it is part of the entire sentence.

   [*Example*: He ran the mile in four minutes (his personal best time)!]

Italics, Underlining, and Quotation Marks
Student Exercise 9

(For rules on quotation marks, see Background Information for Exercise 5.)

1. Underline or italicize titles of books, magazines, newspapers, plays, movies, television series, long poems, paintings, sculptures, long musical compositions, works of art, planes, spacecraft, and ships.

   (*Example*: I read that article in *Time* magazine. OR I read that article in Time magazine.)

2. Italicize or underline, and capitalize, the words *a, an,* or *the* written at the beginning of a title—but only if they are part of the title.

   (*Examples*: I read the book *A Long Journey Home*.

   I read about it in a *Reader's Digest* issue.)

3. Use italics or underlining for foreign words not used commonly in English.

   (*Example*: She has a certain *savoir faire*.)

   Do not use italics or underlining if the foreign word is commonly used.

   (*Example*: He brought me a bouquet.)

4. Use italics or underlining for words, letters, and figures referred to as such.

   (*Examples*: The words *its* and *it's* are often misused.

   The *'s* in your paper must be replaced.)

Numbers and Numerals
Exercise 10

1. To form the plural of numbers used to represent themselves, add an *'s*. The number, but not the apostrophe and *s*, should be italicized or underlined.

   (*Example*: Your *4*'s all look like *9*'s.)

2. In formal or scholarly writing, spell out numbers that can be written in one or two words.

   (*Example*: There are fifty states in the United States.)

3. Spell out any number that comes at the beginning of a sentence.

   (*Example*: Fourteen boys are on the team.)

4. Use numerals to write numbers that have more than two words.

   (*Example*: There are 5,280 feet in a mile.)

5. Very large numbers may be written as a numeral followed by a word such as *million* or *billion*.

   (*Example:* The sun is 93 million miles from the earth.)

6. Use numerals to write amounts of money, decimals, or percentages.

   (*Examples:* He got 90% of the answers right. She weighs 89 pounds.)

7. If an amount of money can be written in one or two words, it should be spelled out.

   (*Example:* He had only two dollars left.)

8. Use numbers to show the year and day in a date.

   (*Example:* He was born on July 4, 1999.)

9. Use numerals to show an exact time, but spell out times that do not use A.M. or P.M.

   (*Examples:* 3:14 A.M., five o'clock)

10. Use numerals for street names over ten and for all house, room, or apartment numbers. Spell out numbered streets of ten or under.

    (*Examples:* 25th Street, Third Avenue, Apartment 3G)

11. Use numerals for pages, acts, lines, or scene numbers.

    (*Example:* Act 2, Scene 3 can be found on page 114. Please memorize lines 12–20.)

Abbreviations
Student Exercise 11

1. Use only one period if an abbreviation comes at the end of a sentence. If the sentence that ends in an abbreviation should end with a question mark or exclamation point, use both punctuation marks.

   (*Examples:* My doctor is John Coleman, M.D.

   Is your doctor's name John Coleman, M.D.?)

2. When abbreviations are formed from the first letters of several words, omit the periods and use all capital letters.

   (*Examples:* We are members of the YMCA.

   CBS, NBC, and ABC are all television networks.)

3. Abbreviations related to time and dates are capitalized.

   (*Examples:* 200 B.C., 5:15 A.M., 6:02 P.M.)

4. Capitalize abbreviations of proper nouns.

   (*Example:* The U.S. Congress is in session.)

5. Postal abbreviations are written with two capital letters and no periods.

   (*Example:* MT is the postal abbreviation for Montana.)

6. Personal titles are usually abbreviated.

   (*Example:* Dr. Smith is not in his office today.)

7. Abbreviate units of measure used with numerals in scientific writing. Do not abbreviate them in ordinary writing. Do not add *s* to these abbreviations.

   (*Example:* The board measured 12 ft. 3 in. The board was about 12 feet long.)

8. Do not use periods after abbreviations of units in the metric system.

   (*Example:* Add 3 g salt to 2 ml water.)

Subject-Verb Agreement
Student Exercise 15

1. Use a singular verb with a singular subject.
   (*Example:* That <u>tree</u> <u>is</u> a Japanese maple.)

2. Use a plural verb with a plural subject.
   (*Example:* <u>Roses</u> <u>are</u> the favorite flowers of many gardeners.)

3. The number of the subject is not changed by a phrase following the subject.
   (*Example:* <u>Roses</u>, unlike the hosta <u>grow</u> best in full sun.)

4. These pronouns are singular: *each, either, neither, one, everyone, everybody, no one, nobody, anyone, anybody, someone,* and *somebody.*
   (*Example:* <u>Each</u> of us <u>likes</u> a different sport.)

5. These pronouns are plural: *several, few, both,* and *many.*
   (*Example:* <u>Several</u> of us <u>are</u> going to the game.)

6. These pronouns may be singular or plural: *some, all, most, any,* or *none.*

(*Examples:* <u>Most</u> of us <u>like</u> this chocolate dessert.

<u>Some</u> of this bread <u>is</u> moldy.

<u>Some</u> of these lentils <u>are</u> not cooked.)

7. Subjects joined by *and* take a plural verb.

(*Example:* <u>Raoul and Elena are</u> on the track team.)

8. Singular subjects joined by *or* or *nor* take singular verbs.

(*Example:* <u>Joe or Henry is</u> going to be my date.)

9. If a singular subject and a plural subject are joined by *or* or *nor,* the verb agrees with the subject closer to the verb.

(*Example:* Craig or <u>the boys are</u> going to mow the lawn today.)

10. If an amount of money refers to one unit, it is singular. If it refers to the individual units, it is plural.

(*Examples:* <u>Twenty-five dollars is</u> too much for that shirt.

<u>Twenty-five dollars are</u> in that envelope.)

11. *Every a* or *many a* before a subject calls for a singular verb.

(*Example:* Many a <u>tear has</u> to fall, but it's all in the game.)

12. A title is singular, even if it ends in a plural noun.

(*Example:* The book <u>*Great Expectations*</u> <u>features</u> the mysterious girl Estella.)

Principal Parts of Verbs
Student Exercise 16

1. All English verbs have four principal parts: a base form, a present participle, the simple past form, and a past participle.

(*Example:* jump, jumping, jumped, have jumped)

2. A regular verb forms its past and past participle by adding *ed* to the base form.

There may be spelling changes when the *ed* is added:

(*Examples:* spy, spied

flop, flopped

argue, argued)

3. An irregular verb forms its past and past participle in some way other than by adding *ed* to the base form.

(*Examples:* lie, lying, lay, have lain

rise, rising, rose, have risen)

Consistent Verb Tense
Student Exercise 17

1. Do not change verb tense when two or more events happened at the same time.

[*Examples:* She forgot her watch, so she came home late. (both past)]

He hurries to the table and gulps his breakfast. (both present)]

2. Change tenses to show that one event came before another.

(*Example:* When we arrived, the play had already started.)

3. Use the present tense to make a statement about a general truth or fact, even if the rest of the sentence is in the past tense.

(*Example:* Gio forgot that seven times eight is fifty-six.)

Case of Personal Pronouns
Student Exercise 18

1. Use the nominative pronouns (*I, he, she, we,* and *they*) as subjects or predicate nominatives.

(*Example:* He and I went skating.)

2. Objective pronouns (*me, him, her, us,* and *them*) should be used only as objects. If the direct object is made up of a noun and a pronoun, the objective pronoun must still be used.

(*Example:* Mrs. Hill helped Bill and me.)

3. When speaking of yourself and others, mention yourself last.

(*Example:* "Shanika and I," not "me and Shan-ika")

4. Don't use an apostrophe in possessive personal pronouns like *my, mine, her, his, hers, its, ours, our, your, yours, their,* or *theirs.*

   [*Example:* The dog chased its tail. (not *it's*)]

5. Verbs must agree with their pronoun subjects.

   [*Example:* He doesn't live here. (not: He don't live here.)]

6. Use the nominative case of a personal pronoun after any form of the verb "to be."

   (*Example:* It is she.)

7. Use possessive pronouns before gerunds (*-ing* forms used as nouns).

   (*Example:* Your yelling bothers me.)

Pronoun-Antecedent Agreement
Student Exercise 19

1. A pronoun must agree with its antecedent in number and gender. (*Number* means singular or plural; *gender* means male, female, or neuter. *Antecedent* means the noun to which the pronoun refers.)

   [*Examples:* <u>She</u> worked hard to get <u>her</u> high school diploma. (she, her—both female)

   <u>She and her brother</u> worked hard to get <u>their</u> diplomas. (plural)]

2. A pronoun must agree in person with its antecedent.

   [*Examples:* <u>Sara</u> is going to the beach, where <u>you</u> can get a tan. (incorrect)

   <u>Sara</u> is going to the beach, where <u>she</u> can get a tan. (correct)]

3. Use a singular, personal pronoun when the antecedent is a singular, indefinite pronoun.

   [*Examples:* <u>Each</u> of the boys must buy <u>their</u> own uniform. (incorrect)

   <u>Each</u> of the boys must buy <u>his</u> own uniform. (correct)]

4. Use a plural verb when the antecedent is a plural, indefinite pronoun.

   [*Examples:* <u>Both</u> of the boys already <u>has</u> uniforms. (incorrect)

   <u>Both</u> of the boys already <u>have</u> uniforms. (correct)]

Clear Pronoun Reference
Student Exercise 20

1. State the antecedent clearly when you use the pronouns *this, that, which,* and *it.*

   [*Examples:* A forest fire spread, which started from a careless camper. (incorrect)

   A forest fire, which was started by a careless camper, spread. (correct)]

2. Make sure a pronoun cannot refer to more than one antecedent.

   [*Example:* When the <u>boy</u> lost sight of his <u>father,</u> <u>he</u> cried. (Who cried?)]

Dangling or Misplaced Modifiers
Student Exercise 22

1. A dangling modifier is a modifying phrase or clause that does not clearly or sensibly modify any word in the sentence. When a modifying phrase begins a sentence, it should be followed by a comma, and then the word that the phrase modifies.

   [*Examples:* Playing football, my leg was hurt. (incorrect)

   Playing football, I hurt my leg. (correct)

   Scrubbing the floor, the baby woke up. (incorrect)]

   Scrubbing the floor, I woke up the baby. (correct)]

2. Modifying phrases and clauses should be placed as near as possible to the words they modify. Otherwise, the meaning of the sentence can be distorted. The modifier can appear to modify the wrong word or more than one word in the sentence.

   [*Examples:* On the stove I saw the soup boiling over. (incorrect)

   I saw the soup boiling over on the stove. (correct)]

Sentence Fragments and Run-on Sentences
Student Exercise 23

1. A sentence fragment may lack a subject, a verb, or both.

    [*Examples:* Jumped across the room. (no subject)

    The entire sixth grade class. (no verb)

    Across town on the subway. (no subject or verb)]

2. A fragment may sometimes be corrected by correct punctuation.

    [*Examples:* I enjoy swimming. Especially in the summer. (incorrect)

    I enjoy swimming, especially in the summer. (correct)]

3. Fragments may incorrectly contain the infinitive or participle form of a verb.

    [*Examples:* Harry hurrying all day long. (incorrect)

    Harry hurried all day long. (correct)

    Erin to be the secretary of the group. (incorrect)

    Erin will be the secretary of the group. (correct)]

4. A run-on sentence is two or more complete sentences written as though they were one sentence.

    a. Two or more sentences may *not* be written without punctuation marks or conjunctions (joining words) between them.

    [*Examples:* We have a long weekend we are so excited. (incorrect)

    We have a long weekend. We are so excited! (correct)

    We have a long weekend; we are so excited! (correct)

    We have a long weekend, and we are so excited! (correct)]

    b. Two or more sentences may not be connected with a comma. (This is known as a "comma splice.")

    [*Examples:* I am hungry, it's time for lunch. (incorrect)

    I am hungry. It's time for lunch. (correct)

    I am hungry; it's time for lunch. (correct)

    I am hungry because it's time for lunch. (correct)]

    c. A comma is used before a coordinating conjunction joining two main clauses.

    [*Examples:* It is Friday and I have to work late. (incorrect)

    It is Friday, and I have to work late. (correct)]

Varying Sentence Styles
Student Exercise 24

1. Vary the kinds of sentences you write, using simple, compound, and complex sentences. Using all simple sentences makes writing seem choppy.
2. Vary sentence length as you write, avoiding too many short sentences and too many long, strung-out sentences.
3. Vary the beginnings of your sentences. Avoid putting the subject first in every sentence. Sometimes start with a modifying word, phrase, or clause.

Using Interesting Language
Student Exercise 25

1. Use interesting synonyms for tired adjectives such as *nice, wonderful, great* . . .
2. Use specific rather than general words to create a picture for the reader.

    [*Examples:* The cat jumped on its toy. (general)

    The tiny, black kitten pounced on the catnip-filled toy mouse. (specific)]

3. Use strong, rather than weak, verbs.

    [*Examples:* She said, "Help!" (weak);

    She screamed, "Help!" (strong)]

4. Avoid using tired clichés and trite expressions. Clichés are words or expressions that are so overused they have lost their meaning and effectiveness. Examples of these are: *busy as a bee, like bumps on a log, teach an old dog new tricks, get the ball rolling.*

Avoiding Wordiness
Student Exercise 26

1. Do not use double negatives.

   [*Examples:* He don't never go there. (incorrect)

   He doesn't ever go there. (correct)]

2. Eliminate superfluous words.

   [*Examples:* In my opinion I think that is right. (wordy)

   In my opinion that is right. (better)]

3. Avoid unnecessary repetition of ideas.

   [*Examples:* In the winter I like to go ice skating in the winter. (repetitious)

   In the winter I like to go ice skating. (better)]

4. Some clauses and phrases may be reduced to fewer words.

   [*Examples:* I have a friend who is a native of Mexico.

   I have a Mexican friend. (better)]

5. Avoid writing in an unnatural, overwritten style. Too many big words, foreign words, flowery phrases, etc., make writing awkward and hard to understand.

   [*Examples:* Illumination is required to be extinguished upon vacating these premises. (wordy)

   Turn out the light when you leave. (better)]

Making Comparisons Correctly
Student Exercise 27

1. Most adverbs and adjectives have three degrees: the base form, the comparative, and the superlative. The comparative is used to compare two things; the superlative three or more.

   (*Example:* I am tall. My brother is taller. My dad is the tallest of the three of us.)

2. For most one-syllable adverbs and adjectives, add *-er* to form the comparative and *-est* to form the superlative.

   (*Example:* black, blacker, blackest)

3. Sometimes spelling changes are needed when adding *-er* and *-est.*

   [*Examples:* big, bigger, biggest (doubling the *g*)

   blue, bluer, bluest (dropping an *e*)

   dry, drier, driest (changing the *y* to *i* before adding the ending)]

4. With most two-syllable adjectives, add *-er* or *-est* to make comparisons.

   (*Examples:* pretty, prettier, prettiest)

5. Use *more* or *most* to form the comparative or superlative of an adverb that ends in *ly.*

   (*Example:* I can see more clearly with my new glasses.)

6. If an adjective or adverb has three or more syllables, always use *more* or *most* to form the comparative or superlative.

   (*Example:* She is even more beautiful than I remembered.)

7. The comparative and superlative forms of some adverbs and adjectives are made irregularly.

   (*Example:* good, better, best)

8. Do not make double comparisons by using both *more* or *most* and *-ed* or *-est* at the same time.

   [*Examples:* She was the most tallest girl in the class. (incorrect)

   She was the tallest girl in the class. (correct)]

9. Avoid incomplete comparisons. These occur when the words *other* or *else* are left out of the comparison.

   [*Examples:* A diamond is harder than any mineral. (This is not clear because it cannot be harder than itself.)

   A diamond is harder than any other mineral. (better)]

10. Avoid illogical comparisons.

   [*Examples:* A piranha's teeth are sharper than
   a man. (What about a man?)

   A piranha's teeth are sharper than a
   man's (teeth).]

11. Always use *good* as an adjective. *Well* can be
   used as an adverb telling how well something
   was done or as an adjective meaning "in good
   health."

   [*Examples:* You did a good job. (correct use as
   an adjective)

   You did good on that test. (incorrect)

   You did well on that test. (correct)

   Do you feel well today? (correct)]

12. Always use *bad* as an adjective. Use *badly* as
   an adverb.

   [*Examples:* She has a bad cold. (correct)

   She did bad on the test. (incorrect)

   She did badly on the test. (correct)]

Correct Usage
Student Exercise 28

The following is a list of words and phrases that may
present usage problems:

advice—(noun) Opinion about how to solve a problem

advise—(verb) To give advice to

a lot—A large number of

alot—This is not a word

awhile—(adverb) For some time

a while—(noun) A period of time

accept—(verb) To agree

except—(preposition) But OR (verb) To leave out

affect—(verb) To influence

effect—(noun) Result OR —(verb) To make happen

ain't—Nonstandard usage. Do not use this word.

all ready—Completely ready

already—Done in the past

all right—O.K.

alright—Incorrect spelling of *all right*. Do not use.

allowed—Permitted

aloud—Out loud

all together—In a group or collectively

altogether—Completely or thoroughly

among—Used to discuss three or more persons or
things

between—Used to discuss two persons or things

bad—Always an adjective. Use after linking verbs.

badly—Always an adverb

beside—Next to

besides—In addition to

breath—(noun) Air breathed into and out of the
lungs

breathe—(verb) To inhale and exhale air

bust, busted—Nonstandard. Do not use these words
to mean to break or burst.

capital—Capital city; capital letter; wealth

capitol—Building in which a legislature meets

choose—(verb) To select or pick out

chose—(verb) Past tense of choose

coarse—(adjective) Not smooth; rough

course—(noun) A course of study; a direction

councilor—(noun) A member of a council

counselor—(noun) A person who gives advise or
guidance

could of, might of—Do not use these phrases. Use
could have or *might have*.

dear—Loved and cherished

deer—An animal

different from, than—Use *different from*, not
different than.

dew—Water droplets condensed from the air

due—Owed or owing

emigrate—To move from one country to another to
live

immigrate—To come to another country to live

fair—Conforming to the rules

fare—A payment

farther—Refers to physical distance

further—Refers to a greater extent in time or degree;
additional

fewer—Used to refer to things that can be counted
individually

less—Used to refer to quantities that cannot be
counted

former—Used to refer to the first of two things
mentioned before

latter—Used to refer to the second of two things mentioned before

good—Always used as an adjective

well—Used as an adverb meaning capably or satisfactorily

hole—An open place, gap, or space

whole—Entire; all

irregardless—Nonstandard. Do not use.

regardless—In spite of everything; anyway

its—A possessive pronoun

it's—A contraction meaning "it is"

isle—Island

aisle—Passageway between row of seats

lay—To put or place something somewhere

lie—To rest or recline

loose—(adjective) Not tight; free

lose—(verb) To fail to keep or find

may be—(verb) Indicates possibility

maybe—(adverb) Perhaps

passed—(verb) Past or past participle of *pass*

past—Having existed at an earlier time

peace—Absence of war or other hostilities

piece—A part of a whole

precede—To go or come before

proceed—To go forward with something

principal—First in rank or importance; leader of a school

principle—Rule, standard

raise—To lift or make something go upward

rise—To move upward

reason is because—Wordy. Do not use this phrase.

reason is that—Because

respectfully—With respect; showing respect

respectively—Each in the order named

said—Past tense of *say*

says—Present tense of *say*

set—To place something

sit—To rest in an upright position

than—(conjunction) Used in comparisons

then—(adverb) Used to show a sequence of events

their—Possessive form of *they*

there—Used to indicate a place; at or in a place

they're—Contraction of *they are*

weather—Activity of the atmosphere at a given time or place

whether—(conjunction) Used to introduce one of two alternatives

who's—Contraction for *who is*

whose—Possessive form of *who*

your—Possessive pronoun

you're—Contraction for *you are*

Answer Key

Find the Errors! II *Pretest*

1. Our American literature class visited Rowan Oak, the Oxford, Mississippi, home of the well-known writer William Faulkner, author of the book *The Sound and the Fury.*

2. Our teacher, Mr. C.J. Cobb, Jr., told us that we would have a school holiday on Columbus Day, and we all yelled "Hooray!"

3. On the biology exam, the students' grades included 8 A's, 7 B's, and 6 C's; however, the teacher was not satisfied with their performance.

4. The suspect was described as a 5'10" male weighing 150 pounds with a heavy, black mustache.

5. Each of the three boys has his own bedroom, which means they don't ever fight.

6. Yoku went to the refrigerator, saw it was empty, and made out a shopping list.

   OR Yoku goes to the refrigerator, sees it is empty, and makes out a shopping list.

7. Reese is going to Glacier National Park, where he can go hiking and fishing.

8. Keri and Ken like to cook, especially on the weekends, when they have extra time.

9. The Nile River, nearly 4,160 miles long, is the longest river in the world.

10. Sojourner Truth, born a slave in New York in the late 18th century, fought against slavery.

11. In the winter I enjoy sports such as skiing and ice skating.

12. The teeth of a crocodile are sharper than a human's.

13. Twelve-year-old Sara and her friends sat all together at the movie, sharing a huge box of popcorn among them, talking a lot, and doing everything except watching the movie. ("Among them" may also be eliminated as redundant, given the use of the word sharing.)

14. She might have passed the algebra exam, but she may be in trouble with her science test, because she forgot about the latter.

15. Jens told his teacher, Mr. Winfield, that his dog ate his homework. When the teacher looked disbelieving, Jens said, "He didn't want to, but I made him."

Misspelled words: author, their, refrigerator, century, all together, a lot, except, passed, may be, latter.

Pretest Error Analysis

1. capitalization, italics, commas, spelling
2. capitalization, abbreviations, quotation marks, commas
3. commas, apostrophes, usage/spelling, semicolons
4. misplaced modifier
5. subject-verb agreement, double negative, commas
6. consistent verb tenses, commas
7. capital letters, commas, pronoun usage
8. sentence fragments, commas
9. run-on sentences, commas, capital letters
10. combining short, choppy sentences; capital letters; commas; spelling
11. avoiding wordiness
12. pronoun reference
13. hyphens, usage, commas, spelling
14. usage errors, commas, spelling
15. quotation marks, capitalization, commas, abbreviations

1. Capital Letters I

   Two friends, Han and Jed, from Boston, Massachusetts, planned a trip together every spring break. One year they went to Orlando, Florida, where they stayed at the Disney Hotel and enjoyed Disney World for three days. Another year they went to New York City, where they saw the play *Hamlet*, ate in the restaurant The Four Seasons, and visited the Empire State Building. This year for a change they decided to go camping in the Rocky Mountains of Montana.

   From L.L. Green Company, they purchased a two-man dome tent that had been highly rated by *Consumer Reports* magazine. They bought Coleman sleeping bags and Swiss Army knives. The rest of their equipment they were able to borrow from Jed's dad. They pored over the guidebook *Camping in the Wilds* by N.A. Tent for advice on making the trip more fun.

   On Saturday, March 15, spring break began. The boys climbed into their old Volkswagen van to begin the drive. By driving all night, they were able to arrive at <u>C</u>lark's <u>F</u>ork of the <u>Y</u>ellowstone <u>R</u>iver by <u>M</u>onday. They pitched their tent and made camp.

The boys began to do some fly-fishing for rainbow trout. It wasn't long before they noticed the huge <u>mosquitoes</u> swarming about. "They're as big as <u>B</u>-1 <u>b</u>ombers," <u>J</u>ed cried, applying a heavy dose of <u>O</u>ff <u>insecticide</u>.

"No, more like the <u>C</u>oncorde," <u>H</u>an replied. "By the way, did you know that the <u>chief</u> enemy of the mosquito is fish like the brown, rainbow, and cutthroat trout?"

After a delicious meal of fried trout and <u>B</u>eanie <u>W</u>eenies, the boys decided to call it a day. They carefully adjusted their <u>R</u>epel brand mosquito netting and climbed into their bags. Nonetheless, a number of intrepid mosquitoes found them. A spraying of insecticide finally <u>abated</u> the attack. A few minutes later, <u>H</u>an noticed some fireflies.

He said to his friend, "<u>W</u>e might as well give up, <u>J</u>ed; those mosquitoes are looking for us with flashlights now!"

SPELLING BOX:	1. advice	2. mosquitoes
3. insecticide	4. chief	5. abated

2. Capital Letters II

<u>J</u>udie was attending a <u>C</u>hristmas party at the home of <u>D</u>r. <u>C</u>.<u>J</u>. <u>C</u>obb, <u>m</u>ayor of <u>H</u>azlehurst, <u>A</u>labama. It was the <u>S</u>aturday before <u>C</u>hristmas, and <u>J</u>udie had attended a number of lavish affairs, one with <u>M</u>exican food, one with <u>I</u>talian food and another with traditional <u>A</u>merican food. <u>J</u>udie now had an extra ten pounds to show for it.

<u>J</u>udie struck up a conversation with a young woman named <u>I</u>la <u>M</u>. <u>S</u>lim. <u>I</u>la, a graduate of <u>A</u>labama <u>S</u>tate, began talking about her job. "<u>Y</u>ou know, it's sad," she said. "<u>S</u>o many people these days are out of work, and here <u>I</u> am living off the fat of the land."

"<u>H</u>ow do you do that?" <u>J</u>udie asked.

"<u>I</u>'m an aerobics <u>instructor</u> at <u>W</u>ebster's <u>G</u>ym in the <u>S</u>ears <u>B</u>uilding," she replied. "<u>C</u>ome join us in <u>J</u>anuary. <u>W</u>e are starting a new aerobics group."

<u>J</u>udie was afraid she would look huge among all the svelte women wearing their spandex <u>S</u>peedo workout clothes. But she had made a <u>N</u>ew <u>Y</u>ear's resolution to lose <u>weight</u>. So on <u>J</u>anuary 2, she

hopped in her <u>T</u>oyota and took <u>H</u>ighway 51 to <u>W</u>ebster's <u>G</u>ym.

<u>A</u>rriving at the gym, she chose an <u>A</u>cme treadmill in the far west corner of the room, hoping to be inconspicuous. <u>S</u>he worked out for ten minutes. <u>T</u>hen <u>I</u>la arrived, put on a tape of "<u>G</u>o <u>Y</u>ou <u>C</u>hicken <u>F</u>at, <u>G</u>o," and began the 60-minute workout.

<u>J</u>udie tried to keep up, but fell farther and farther behind. It had been a long time since she had taken <u>B</u>ody <u>C</u>onditioning 101 at <u>H</u>endrix <u>C</u>ollege. She saw one person after another turn and <u>stare</u> at her. She hoped it was just her imagination. <u>S</u>he tried to imagine herself somewhere else, like in the <u>R</u>ocky <u>M</u>ountains listening to <u>M</u>ozart. But when one woman turned, stared at her, and squinted to get a better look, Judie wanted to <u>disappear</u>.

<u>J</u>udie stopped her workout and picked up her <u>N</u>ike duffel bag. She hoped to sneak undetected out the west door, which led to the <u>H</u>igh <u>S</u>treet parking lot, and make a swift getaway in her <u>C</u>amry. As she turned, she realized that the gym's only wall clock, a small nine-inch <u>E</u>lgin, had been hanging just inches above her head the entire time.

SPELLING BOX:	1. mayor	2. instructor
3. weight	4. stare	5. disappear

3. Commas I

January 25, 20—

Dear Dad,

Yes, things are going well at school, but they could be better. Last weekend I took Sue out to dinner, the dance, and a movie. My suit was wrinkled, and I had to take it to the cleaners. We tried that cozy, quaint restaurant you mentioned. It was good but expensive. Sue ordered, not surprisingly, the most expensive entrée on the menu. You did say to treat her well, didn't you?

On Tuesday, January 14, I got repairs done on my car. I took it to the shop you <u>recommended</u> at 145 Kings Highway, Bangor, Maine. Dad, it cost fifty dollars for the belts, fifty dollars for <u>labor</u>, and another twenty for the oil change. After looking it over, the mechanic, Keith Crenshaw, said the car is shot. Alarmed by the many things wrong, he fixed only the most <u>essential</u>. Well, you can guess what I really need. I hope you will send some soon.

Your son,

Miguel Olmos, Jr.

January 30, 20—

Dear Son,

Nothing pleases me more than a letter from Northern Maine University. I know you are getting a great education and the ability to solve problems <u>independently</u>. Oh, I guess you are a chip off the old <u>block</u>, aren't you?

Well, nothing much is going on around here. It is <u>almost</u> noon, and your sister is still in bed. No one is awake but me. There is no time like the present to give this letter to the mailman, who will send it your way.

Your dad,

Miguel Olmos, Sr.

SPELLING BOX: 1. recommended   2. labor
3. essential   4. independently   5. almost

---

4. Commas II

Jay had been fishing for walleye, his favorite fish, at a remote lake in Wisconsin all week, and he had had little <u>success</u>. He had tried minnows, lures, and jigs, all to no avail. It had been most discouraging, so he was thinking about packing up and heading for home.

That afternoon he saw a fisherman standing in the lake holding a mirror. Attached to the handle of the mirror was a large net. "Excuse me," Jay said, "but what are you doing?"

"I'm fishing, of <u>course</u>," came the reply.

"With a mirror?" Jay asked, thinking the man was crazy.

"Yep, it's my latest invention, and this time I'm going to make a fortune!" the man said.

"How does it work?" Jay asked, already smelling a fish fry.

"Well, I'll tell you, but it will cost you $100," the man said, appearing <u>reluctant</u> to share his secret.

Jay was anxious to catch some fish to take home, so he reached in his pocket, counted out the money, and handed it to the man.

"O.K.," the fisherman said. "You aim the mirror into the water, and when the fish swims by, the rays of light reflected from the mirror shine right in his eyes. This <u>temporarily</u> blinds the fish, and he begins

to swim in a circle in <u>confusion</u>. Then you simply dip the net into the water, and you grab him with it."

"Oh, that's the dumbest thing I've ever heard! How many have you caught like this?"

"Well, you're the third one today!" answered the fisherman with a smile.

SPELLING BOX: 1. success   2. course
3. reluctant   4. temporarily   5. confusion

---

5. Quotation Marks

A nervous, balding man in his 40's had an <u>appointment</u> to see a <u>counselor</u>. He had never gotten help before, but he told himself that things were so bad he had to do something! He pulled into the parking lot, ignoring the sign that read "Exit Only." The theme song "Titanic" was going around in his head. "I'm really losing it," he told himself with a sinking feeling.

"I'm supposed to go to the door with a sign that says 'Dr. Lucy D. Hope, Therapist,'" he reminded himself. "She told me on the phone, 'You can't miss it.'"

Finding the office an hour later, the man was <u>relieved</u>. "It's a good thing I <u>allowed</u> plenty of time; I'm not even late!" he told himself.

Dr. Hope ushered him into her comfortable office. "What seems to be the problem?" she asked.

"Doctor, I just don't know what to do! It's all more than I can stand," he began.

"Well, just calm down and tell me all about it," she replied. "As I always say, 'A burden shared is a burden lightened.'"

"O.K., Doctor. I have a 5-bedroom home on 3 acres on Lake Caroline in Madison County. I drive a BMW, and my wife drives a Jaguar. I have three children in college, and I bought each of them a new car. We belong to the country club. Each summer we spend a month in Europe."

"Haven't you ever heard the expression 'It's not nice to brag'?" said the counselor. "Let's get back to what is really bothering you."

"Don't you see?" the man shouted. "I only make $700 a month!"

SPELLING BOX: 1. appointment   2. counselor
3. relieved   4. allowed   5. It's

---

6. Hyphens, Colons, and Semicolons

It was a rainy-looking day; the five-year-old boy couldn't find anything to do. His mother suggested the following: video games, coloring, helping in the kitchen, and playing "hide and seek." None of these activities <u>interested</u> the boy; everything was "boring." It was only 10:30 A.M., and the forecast was for all-day thunderstorms. Thunder and <u>lightning</u>, as well as torrents of rain, were coming down from dark-looking clouds.

Finally, the mother hit on a plan. She pulled a well-worn photo album from the shelf. She began showing the boy pictures of long-<u>forgotten</u> times.

"Here is your Uncle Fred. A self-made man, he was well-liked by everyone. And here is Aunt Josie on the day she turned twenty-one. Here is your great-grandmother reading her <u>favorite</u> Bible verse, John 3:16. There are many more pictures here of your brothers, sisters, and other family members. I need to go put the roast in the oven; however, I'll be back in about 10 minutes."

The little boy continued looking through the album. When he was about three- fourths done, he saw someone he didn't <u>recognize</u>.

"Mom," he called. "Who is this red-headed man standing next to Ahn? You know, the curly-haired one with the funny-looking glasses?"

"Why, that's your hard-working father; you know that!" exclaimed his mother.

The boy spent nearly one-half minute puzzling over this all-perplexing problem; however, he was still confused.

"But, Mom," he replied. "If that's Dad, who's that bald-headed man upstairs?"

SPELLING BOX:	1. interested	2. lightning
3. forgotten	4. favorite	5. recognize

7. Apostrophes

Revel Applewhite was a mechanic at Wong's Automotive. Ten years' experience and careful attention to his customers' needs, always minding his *p*'s and *q*'s, had made him the subject of many customers' requests. He even worked on his mother-in-law's car to her satisfaction. It's hard to meet everyone's needs all of the time, but Revel gave it his best shot. He still tells the story of the hard-to-please customer he met in January '03.

Mr. Ortiz brought in his twin daughters' car to be repaired. He told the mechanic, "It's making a very strange noise, then it's stalling."

Revel took the girls' car into his shop. He started the motor and listened to its sound. It would run smoothly for about thirty seconds' time, then stall. Its stalling did not puzzle Revel at all. He took out a small <u>hammer</u> and tapped the engine three times lightly in the same spot. Once again he started the <u>motor</u> and listened to its sound. "Well, it's fixed. I'll <u>mail</u> you a bill," he told Mr. Ortiz.

Two days later, Mr. Ortiz opened the bill from Wong's Automotive. It read:

> For <u>tapping</u> engine with hammer: $1
> For knowing where to tap: $1000
> Total: $1001

Mr. Ortiz' blood pressure went through the roof. He called Revel to make his <u>complaints</u>. "There are too many 0's in this bill! I never heard of such prices since back in '01! It'll be a cold day in July before I'll take my car back to your shop. I'd have replaced the children's car before I'd have agreed to spend all that! That's a week of my pay!"

"Well, if the car's stalling has stopped, the <u>peace</u> of mind should be worth it," Revel replied, accepting the stack of hundreds with a smile.

SPELLING BOX:	1. hammer	2. motor
3. tapping	4. complaints	5. peace

8. Parentheses

A local camping goods store (this large store sells goods for camping in all types of climates and terrain) conducted camping workshops every Monday. One week the topic was "Climbing the Himalayas" (a mountain range in southern Asia). Another week the topic was "Whitewater Rafting in Mississippi." (Mississippi is <u>principally</u> known for its slow-moving creeks, so this topic generated a good deal of curiosity.) "Hiking in the <u>Arctic</u>" was another popular lecture. This Monday (July 16) the topic for the workshop was "<u>Desert</u> Survival." A large group of prospective campers (they ranged in age from 16 to 60) assembled in the store at 7:00 P.M. for the <u>occasion</u>.

"What are the three most important things you should bring with you (put them in order of their importance) in case you get lost in the desert?" the leader asked.

A lot of discussion (some of it was pretty heated) ensued. Everyone seemed to have strong opinions. Finally the group (at least most of them) reached a consensus.

"A compass, a canteen of water, and a deck of cards," answered the spokesperson (the most experienced camper).

"Please explain your choices (aren't your priorities strange?)," the leader replied.

"The compass (as I am sure anyone would know) is to find in which direction you should go. A compass (it is an instrument with a needle that points to the magnetic north pole) is easy to carry in your pocket. After all it's pretty easy to get lost in the desert with so few landmarks to go by. A canteen of water (you can survive only a short time without water, while you can live weeks without food) would be vital (this would be to prevent dehydration)," was the reply.

"What about the deck of cards (an odd idea)?" the leader persisted.

"Well, as soon as you start playing solitaire (which would be a good way to relax after a long day of trudging through the sand) someone is sure to come up behind you and say, 'Put that black ten on the red jack!' And then you're found!"

SPELLING BOX:	1. principally	2. Arctic
3. Desert	4. occasion	5. priorities

9. Italics, Underlining, and Quotation Marks

Be sure students understand that titles that they would underline on a worksheet or handwritten paper may be italicized when the student is using a word processor.

Mrs. Moore's English class was discussing their favorite works of art and literature. It was a lively discussion with everyone in the class participating.

"My favorite painting is Physical Education by Jim Shorts," said Shay.

"I heard a great song called 'Garden Mulch' by the group Peat Moss," said Mary.

"I saw an exciting action movie called Runaway Train last weekend," added Mario. "It was directed by Dee Rail."

Tran raised his hand. "The poem 'Why Dogs Scratch' by Manny Fleas is hilarious," he said.

Alex mentioned that his dad had bought a new cookbook called The Cookout Cookbook by Burntoo A. Crisp.

"There was a terrific article in the magazine Sports Pictured. It was called 'How to Be Great at Sports' by Hugh Da Mann!" offered Tony.

"You know how I love to watch ads on television," Akira broke in. "Well, on Tuesday I saw this great television special called Classic Commercials, directed by Will B. Wrightback."

Gavin said that in the newspaper The Jackson Times he had read an article called "Proofreading" by the famous writer Ty Poe.

The teacher called the class to order. "I think I'll take a week off. I've been reading the article 'Planning a Vacation' by Vera U. Going, and I think I'm ready for a break. Remember, your book reports are due next week. You will find an excellent resource guide in the book Need Help Writing a Book Report? by Philip A. Page. I hope you have a great week with the substitute, Mrs. A. Skeeme. She'll probably fill you all in on the book she's writing called How to Make Money Easily."

SPELLING BOX:	1. favorite	2. literature
3. lively	4. Commercials	5. planning

10. Numbers and Numerals

1. "At five o'clock I asked you to notice when the Sixteen-Bean Soup boiled over."

   "I did, Mom! It boiled over at 6:15 P.M. on October 20, 2004."

2. "Let's say I take seven apples from twelve apples. What's the difference?"

   "That's what I say: What's the difference?"

3. "Why should the number 288 (two hundred eighty-eight) never be mentioned in polite company?"

   "Because it is two gross."(A gross is 144.)

4. "Mr. Green is a butcher who lives in Apartment 8C at 1453 North 66th Street. His shop is at 15 Second Avenue. He is forty years old, six feet tall and wears a size eleven shoe. What does he weigh?"

   "Meat."

5. "What occurs one time in a minute, <u>two</u> times in a moment, but not once in the twentieth <u>century</u>?"

   "The letter *m.*"

6. "How are you doing training your new dog?"

   "Great! Yesterday I taught her to beg. Today she came back with <u>forty-five</u> cents."

SPELLING BOX:	1. notice	2. difference
3. hundred	4. shoe	5. century

11. Abbreviations

1. TX; Mr. A.B. Payton, Jr.; IRS
2. A.M.; FBI; MS; Dept.; N.; Ave.; U.S.
3. ABC; P.M.; I.M. Windy, Ph.D.; Blvd.
4. Sgt.; B.A.; Pvt. I.M.
5. Sen.; A.; Ave.; DC
6. cm; gal.; lbs.; mg

SPELLING BOX:	1. announced	2. leak
3. Professor	4. holes	5. nonsense

12. Review of Punctuation and Capitalization I

<u>R</u>odney and <u>L</u>indsey lived in <u>P</u>alatka, <u>F</u>lorida, a small hamlet in the central part of the state. Since <u>F</u>lorida has a humid, subtropical climate, they were <u>unaccustomed</u> to snow, ice, and cold weather. Not once did they have to get up early to warm the car, scrape ice off the <u>windshield</u>, or watch the weather report on television.

<u>R</u>odney was a twenty-one-year-old self-employed carpenter. Lindsey, a recent high school graduate, was a well-liked teaching <u>assistant</u> in a local elementary school. Both liked their jobs; however, neither was well-paid. They decided to apply for jobs in another state. At 10:30 <u>A.M.</u> on <u>F</u>riday, <u>O</u>ctober 15, the mail arrived at their home at 125 <u>A</u>thens <u>C</u>t., <u>P</u>alatka, <u>F</u>lorida, with exciting news. Both had job offers in <u>B</u>uffalo, <u>N</u>ew <u>Y</u>ork, a spot far distant from <u>F</u>lorida. Being adventurous, they decided to take the jobs.

Soon after they arrived, a big snowstorm hit <u>B</u>uffalo. <u>B</u>eing on the shore of <u>L</u>ake <u>E</u>rie, <u>B</u>uffalo is subject to a phenomenon known, not surprisingly, as the lake effect. Winds blow over the lake, picking up moisture. Hitting the shore, they dump unusually large amounts of precipitation (rain or snow) on the

city. This particular storm dumped nearly two feet of snow on the newcomers' home.

The next morning, as <u>L</u>indsey was backing out of the driveway, her car slid into a ditch. She called a local garage; they sent a tow truck, and she was soon on her way to work at <u>C</u>asey <u>S</u>chool. On her lunch break a few hours later, <u>L</u>indsey got stuck again. The same tow truck rescued her. Finally, at four o'clock, she headed home. However, before she arrived she went off the road again, this time knocking down a mailbox, spinning around, and ending up in yet another ditch. Down the road came the same tow truck; how <u>embarrassing</u>! Nonetheless, she arrived home safe and sound, resolving to learn how to drive better in snow.

Later that night, after <u>R</u>odney and <u>L</u>indsey had eaten, the phone rang, and <u>R</u>odney answered it. "It's the tow truck driver, <u>dear</u>," he called to her. "He wants to know if <u>it's</u> <u>O.K.</u> to put the tow truck away!"

SPELLING BOX:	1. unaccustomed	2. windshield
3. assistant	4. embarrassing	5. dear

13. Review of Punctuation and Capitalization II

Tony was a sixteen-year-old boy, and he had just passed his driver's <u>license</u> exam. Whenever he got the chance, he drove other family members wherever they needed to go.

One day (it was a beautiful day in early <u>M</u>ay), <u>T</u>ony was driving with his grandpa in his grandpa's four-wheel-drive vehicle down a bumpy, dusty, dirt road. He didn't know how to control the car very well; however, he kept on going. A little embarrassed about his poor driving, he decided to make an excuse. "The sun and shadows on the road make it hard to see the potholes," he said lamely.

"Don't worry, my boy," <u>G</u>randpa said. "<u>Y</u>ou're getting most of them!"

Pulling back onto the paved road, <u>T</u>ony began driving faster. <u>U</u>nfortunately, he soon saw flashing blue lights behind him, a sure sign that a patrolman had spotted him speeding. Tony pulled off the road, and he stopped the car. "Sorry officer," he said. "<u>I</u>t's my grandpa's car, and it doesn't have <u>cruise</u> control."

The trooper stuck his head in the window, looking for the dashboard. "<u>Y</u>oung man," he said gruffly, "it may not have cruise control, but it does have a speedometer." Nonetheless, he let Tony go with a warning, probably due to the boy's youth.

Tony continued home, watching the speed limit carefully. Soon he had gotten over his near miss, and he decided to munch on an apple. It wasn't until he tossed the core out the window that he realized the same police car was still following him. Once again the policeman, in a much sterner mood, pulled Tony over.

Tony joked nervously that he was just trying to clean up the roadside. The apple core, of course, could serve as a home for ants, which would then clean up tiny bits of litter, improving the environment.

Seeing the big, tough trooper cracking a smile, Tony thought he had it made. Then the trooper said, pulling out his ticket book, "O.K., let's see your building permit!"

SPELLING BOX:	1. license	2. cruise
3. due	4. litter	5. environment

14. Review of Punctuation and Capitalization III

1. Lacey was applying for a secretarial job, a position she really wanted. She arrived at the personnel office at 10:30 A.M. on Friday, June 21. While completing the application, she was careful to dot all her i's and cross all her t's. Lacey, a recent graduate of W.B. Murrah High School, really wanted this job! She came to the question, "What would you consider your strengths for this position?" Lacey thought a minute, then answered, "Two of my strengths are spelling and proofreading, and on this application the word 'applicant' is misspelled." Lacey got the job!

2. Abbey, a student in Mrs. A.B. Wright's English class, had the assignment of writing a five-paragraph essay. She chose the following for her topic: "Chivalry (sic) Is Dead." Her teacher returned the paper without Abbey's hoped-for A's or B's. It not only had the grade of C, but it also had the comment, " 'Chivalry' is not only dead, it is also misspelled."

3. The high school English teacher, Mr. J.W. Barfield, had been explaining the ins and outs of grammar and punctuation for weeks. In fact, the month's lessons had contained little else,

much to the students' dismay (they found it boring).

Finally, the lesson plan switched to poetry, a welcome change for the students. One day, as the class was reading the works of a modern poet, one student seemed puzzled. "I don't get it, Mr. Barfield," he said. "How come the poet uses no capital letters and misspells some of the words?"

"That's called poetic license," Mr. Barfield explained.

"Oh," the young man replied, appearing relieved. "How can I apply for one?"

SPELLING BOX:	1. personnel	2. applicant
3. Chivalry	4. misspelled	5. relieved

15. Subject-Verb Agreement

Three women, Jena, Yolanda, and Ann, were shipwrecked on a deserted island. Each of them (was, were) without any supplies or extra clothing. Several coconut trees (was, were) growing nearby to provide shade and food. A small spring, surrounded by mossy rocks, (was, were) a source of fresh water.

Jena, along with Yolanda, (was, were) the adventurous sort. She decided to explore the island. Neither (was, were) able to persuade Ann to join them. As far as Jena was concerned, boredom, as well as the poor selection of food, (was, were) reason enough to explore their environs. Besides, sunbathing, as well as recovering from the ordeal of the wreck, (was, were) getting to be boring.

Both Jena and Yolanda (was, were) eager to begin. They (was, were) able to circumvent the perimeter of the island in just under forty minutes. Neither rocks nor an extremely high tide (was, were) able to slow them down.

The next of their options (was, were) to climb the hill on the north side of the island. It was a pleasant climb; both wildflowers and tall grasses (was, were) plentiful. But neither food nor supplies (was, were) to be found.

Suddenly, Yolanda, the more observant of the two, (was, were) overcome with excitement. On the ground, nearly hidden in the tall grasses, (was, were) a brass lamp. The lamp, in both shape and color, (was, were) exactly like the famed Aladdin's lamp. Both Yolanda and Jena (was, were) in agreement on hurrying back to show Ann the lamp.

Jena rubbed the lamp, and everyone (<u>was</u>, were) surprised when a genie appeared! Each woman (<u>was</u>, were) granted one wish. Yolanda went first. Her wish (<u>was</u>, were) for a helicopter, and she flew away, <u>disappearing</u> into the sky. Jena, unlike the others, (<u>was</u>, were) not <u>entirely</u> afraid of boats, so she wished for a sailboat and <u>sailed</u> away. Ann was lonely, so her wish (<u>was</u>, were) for her two friends to return.

SPELLING BOX:	1. deserted	2. forty
3. extremely	4. disappearing	5. entirely

16. Principal Parts of Verbs

Mr. Bishop had just (got, <u>gotten</u>) back from a wonderful three-week vacation in Australia. He had (ate, <u>eaten</u>) a lot of fabulous seafood and had (drank, <u>drunk</u>) some of the fine local wines. Each day he had (rise, rose, <u>risen</u>) early and had (ate, <u>eaten</u>) a large breakfast. After this, he had (lay, <u>lain</u>, laid) down for a brief nap. Soon he had (sat, <u>set</u>) out for the day's adventure.

On the way home, Mr. Bishop (<u>sat</u>, set) on the plane for 16 hours. He (lay, <u>laid</u>) the seat back as far as it would go. Nonetheless, he (<u>slept</u>, sleep) very little. He was able to (<u>take</u>, took) full advantage of the <u>personal service</u> and fine meals offered.

Needless to say, when Mr. Bishop arrived home, he found that his weight had (rose, <u>risen</u>) about 10 pounds. He was <u>embarrassed</u> and sorry he had (<u>set</u>, sit) foot on the scales! But he (goed, <u>went</u>) in to the doctor for advice. The doctor put him on a diet.

"I want you to eat normally for two days, then skip a day," the doctor (<u>told</u>, telled) him sternly. "Repeat this procedure for two weeks. Your weight should have (shrank, <u>shrunk</u>) considerably by then. You should have (<u>lost</u>, losed) five pounds."

When Mr. Bishop (<u>went</u>, gone) back to the doctor two weeks later, he (steps, <u>stepped</u>) on the scales. Sure enough, he had (loose, <u>lost</u>) ten pounds! "<u>All right</u>!" he exclaimed.

"A <u>noticeable</u> improvement! Did you follow my directions?" the doctor asked.

Mr. Bishop nodded. "But it (<u>wasn't</u>, weren't) easy. I (think, <u>thought</u>) I was going to faint on each third day."

"From hunger?" (asks, <u>asked</u>) the doctor.

"No," Mr. Bishop (<u>said</u>, says). "From skipping!"

SPELLING BOX:	1. personal	2. service
3. embarrassed	4. all right	5. noticeable

17. Consistent Verb Tense

The verbs in this story have all been changed to the past tense. (An alternative would be to change every verb to present tense.)

Maggie, a high school student, ask<u>ed</u> her father, "Dad, can you sign your name with your eyes closed?"

Her dad was perplexed. "I guess so. Why, dear?"

"My report card came in the mail today," she answer<u>ed</u>.

Maggie's dad <u>was</u> not happy when he <u>saw</u> her grades. Her math grade was a C, but she <u>had</u> D's in all her other classes.

They <u>sat</u> down to talk about her study habits. Maggie maintain<u>ed</u> that she studied at least two hours every night. Maggie's dad decided to observe her study habits the following night. He plan<u>ned</u> to determine what changes she might make to improve her efficiency and <u>achieve</u> better grades.

Maggie's study time was from 7 to 9 P.M., and she follow<u>ed</u> this <u>schedule</u> carefully. Here is how she us<u>ed</u> her time that night:

For 15 minutes she look<u>ed</u> for the <u>piece</u> of paper on which she had <u>written</u> her assignments. It <u>took</u> 17 minutes for her to call a friend to get the assignment plus the latest news. Two trips to the bathroom add<u>ed</u> up to 10 more minutes. It was important to keep up her strength, so Maggie <u>spent</u> 12 minutes concocting a snack in the kitchen. Maggie check<u>ed</u> the TV schedule in the newspaper. She decided what she would watch after she finish<u>ed</u> her homework. This <u>took</u> another 6 minutes.

Maggie <u>was</u> getting frustrated. She spent 15 minutes <u>complaining</u> that the teacher <u>did</u> not explain the assignment. Another 20 minutes elapsed as Maggie complain<u>ed</u> about the teacher. Maggie <u>said</u> she was mean and <u>did</u> not understand kids.

Maggie finally <u>sat</u> down at her desk and looked at her book. She thumb<u>ed</u> through a stack of paper for 15 minutes. For the final 10 minutes of the study period, Maggie <u>tried</u> to get her dad to do the work for her. At 9 P.M. sharp, Maggie clos<u>ed</u> her books, turned on the TV and said, "You've got to <u>admit</u>, Dad, I worked pretty hard tonight!"

18. Case of Personal Pronouns

1. Boss: "How come (you and Bill, Bill and yourself) are only carrying one sack when the other men are carrying two?"

   Worker: "I suppose (its, it's) because (they are, their) too lazy to make two trips the way (Bill and me, Bill and I) do."

2. Boss: "I'd like to go through one whole day without scolding (you and he, you and him)."

   Worker: "Well, you certainly have (my, mine) consent."

3. Worker #1: "I told (our, our's) boss that (you and me, you and I) are perfect."

   Worker #2: "Did (she, her) agree with you?"

   Worker #1: "I don't know. She (haven't, hasn't) stopped laughing at (I, me) yet!"

4. For years, Mr. Allen's secretary was fifteen minutes late to work every day. Then one morning (she, her) was only ten minutes late. Mr. Allen remarked, "(You, Your) being late bothers me. But this is the earliest you've ever been late to this job of (yours, your's).

5. Worker: My boss was a very tactful man; a master of tact was (he, him). He called me in one day and said, "When the vice president and (me, I) think about it, (we, I) don't know how (we're, were) going to get along without you, but starting Monday, (we're, were) going to try!"

6. Phil and Art were in the stockroom of a large warehouse lounging against a packing crate when the boss came in. Addressing Phil, who was wearing a name tag, the boss asked, "(You, Your) standing around makes me furious! How much are (you and he, you and him) getting a week?"

   "About $200 a week each," came (they're, their) answer.

   "Here's (your, you're) $200 apiece. Now get out of here and don't come back," the boss said angrily.

   Phil and (he, him) put the money in (they're, their) pockets and hurried out.

The boss saw the stockroom manager and called to (he, him), "How long (has, have) (Phil and him, Phil and he) been working here?"

"They don't work here. (Phil and him, Phil and he) just delivered a package!"

19. Pronoun-Antecedent Agreement

Ahmed and his friend Jabbar were from the big city, where they didn't see much green space. They worked hard to plan their camping trip in the wilds of northern Minnesota. It was the first time either of them had been camping. They were going to a remote spot where they could catch lots of fish. They had hired a fishing guide with an excellent reputation they could rely on.

Jabbar and he found the long trip tired them out. First they took an airplane journey (another first for them) to St. Paul. Then came a 200-mile car trip north. Jabbar and he made the last leg of their journey by boat. Both were glad it was a motorboat, not a canoe.

When the two got to the guide's cabin, they went inside. The guide stayed outside to finish some of the chores he had to do. Both were surprised to see the pot-bellied stove in a most unusual position, set up on posts nearly three feet off the cabin floor. Neither of the men knew the reasons for its unusual placement.

Jabbar said, "I'm sure it's for a practical reason. The heat from the stove would dry out green or wet wood placed under it."

"I imagine," said Ahmed, "that the heat from the stove circulates much quicker around the room, thus warming it quicker for you and me."

"Actually," Jabbar replied, warming to his subject, "we both know that warm air rises in a room. Cool air can come in an open window at night so it will not get too hot."

The two men thought hard to get their dilemma figured out. When the guide returned, they asked him to settle the argument for them.

"It's simple," he explained to Ahmed and him. When I brought the stove upriver on my boat, I lost one section of stovepipe overboard. So I set the stove up high so I could get the smoke to go out the hole in the roof!"

SPELLING BOX: 1. excellent   2. practical
3. dilemma   4. argument   5. overboard

20. Clear Pronoun Reference

(There may be more than one correct way to rewrite the sentences to provide clear pronoun references. Accept any reasonable answer.)

1. The teacher told the student that all students were expected to be at school by 8:00 A.M. The student <u>replied</u> that she understood, but the teacher <u>should</u> go ahead without her if the student wasn't there by then!

2. A student was happy when he was reminded that he would have a half day of school that morning. Then he <u>realized</u> that the other half day would be that <u>afternoon</u>!

3. A lecturer's announcement to his audience that the world would end in <u>approximately</u> nine billion years scared one person badly. The frightened person thought the lecturer had said nine *million* years.

4. When an envelope was crossed with a homing pigeon, the letter came back every time it was mailed.

5. In Utah there is a lake that's so clear, when you look into it, you can see people making tea in China.

6. He was the new boss at the cheese factory, and his position was evident in the sign on his desk that read "The Big Cheese."

7. Mark worked as a <u>professional comedian</u>, a laughable job.

SPELLING BOX: 1. replied   2. realized
3. approximately   4. professional   5. comedian

21. Review of Subject-Verb Agreement and Pronouns

Julio and Beth both (has, <u>have</u>) landed new jobs in another city. They (<u>are</u>, is) excited about the move, but first they, like most people in this position, (has, <u>have</u>) to sell their house. The two (cleans, <u>clean</u>) each room until (you, <u>they</u>) can't do any more. Finally, everything (<u>is</u>, are) as <u>perfect</u> as (you, <u>they</u>) can make it.

Beth lists (<u>their</u>, they're) house with a real estate agent, and for a few weeks the agent works hard for Julio and (<u>her</u>, she). Julio and Beth (<u>become</u>, becomes)

obsessive housekeepers. Every dish (<u>has</u>, have) to be washed <u>immediately</u>. Each piece of clothing (<u>has</u>, have) to be hung up or put away. The carpets (is, <u>are</u>) <u>vacuumed</u> daily. Every particle of dust (<u>is</u>, are) removed. Every room (<u>has</u>, have) to be perfect at all times. After all, no one (<u>is</u>, are) sure when a prospective buyer might show up at (<u>their</u>, they're) door.

Then one day, the doorbell (ring, <u>rings</u>) without warning at 8 A.M. Julio, as well as Beth, (open, <u>opens</u>) the door. There they see (<u>their</u>, they're) real estate agent with a couple from Alaska who (want, <u>wants</u>) to see the house. The agent (<u>doesn't</u>, don't) make much of an <u>apology</u>. He says that there had been no time to call. The Alaskans (has, <u>have</u>) to catch a <u>plane</u> in an hour.

So, three people (<u>make</u>, makes) (<u>their</u>, they're) way through the kitchen which (<u>is</u>, are) dirty and full of dishes. Next stop: the bedroom with (<u>its</u>, it's) unmade beds! Several towels (is, <u>are</u>) strewn across the bathroom floor. Beth, as well as Julio, (<u>is</u>, are) still in a bathrobe. In addition, Beth (<u>is</u>, are) sporting curlers in her hair. The whole picture (<u>doesn't</u>, don't) at all give the image the couple (hope, <u>hopes</u>) to present. They don't remember (<u>ever</u>, never) being so embarrassed!

The next day, the real estate agent (phone, <u>phones</u>) Julio to say that the couple from Alaska (<u>has</u>, have) bought the house! He then told Beth and (he, <u>him</u>) what the buyer had said about the house: "That house, of all the ones we looked at, (<u>has</u>, have) a warm, lived-in look, just like ours!"

SPELLING BOX: 1. perfect   2. immediately
3. vacuumed   4. apology   5. plane

22. Dangling or Misplaced Modifiers

(Answers may vary somewhat; accept all reasonable answers.)

1. The bride, wearing her mother's wedding <u>veil</u>, was given away by her father.

2. The <u>amateur</u> photographer captured some beautiful autumn leaves falling from a tree.

3. Writing all night long, I finally finished the term paper.

4. The repairman with the helpful smile arrived to fix the air conditioner.

5. With his <u>binoculars</u>, the bird-watcher saw the two birds fighting.

6. After I took a shower, the bed looked inviting to me.
7. I saw one of his <u>campaign</u> signs nailed to a telephone pole.
8. The sign at the movies read: "No children under eight years of age <u>admitted</u> without an adult."
9. The plane took off on time after I had eaten a rushed breakfast.

SPELLING BOX:	1. veil	2. amateur
3. binoculars	4. campaign	5. admitted

23. Sentence Fragments and Run-on Sentences

(There will be more than one acceptable way to correct these sentences. Accept all correct variations.)

A couple was driving through a deserted area of Wyoming. The ground was flat, and the road was straight. There was not another car in sight for miles. The weather was perfect: blue <u>skies</u> and not a cloud in sight.

The couple began to drive faster and faster. A policeman <u>suddenly</u> appeared out of nowhere. He pulled them over, his blue lights flashing.

"I'm going to have to give you a ticket," the policeman said sternly. "Driving at one <u>hundred</u> miles per hour is not <u>acceptable</u>."

"That can't be <u>accurate</u>! I've only been driving ten minutes," the man said.

Noticing the couple was wearing seat belts, the trooper began to put his ticket book away. He was going to let them off with a warning.

Then the man (unwisely) added, "Officer, when you drive the speeds I do, you've got to wear a safety belt."

SPELLING BOX:	1. skies	2. suddenly
3. hundred	4. acceptable	5. accurate

24. Varying Sentence Styles

(There is more than one correct way to rewrite this story. Accept any reasonable answers.)

I was driving with my younger brother, who had just gotten his learner's permit. It was the first time he had driven the car since getting his permit.

At first I was pleased to see how well he was handling the busy road. After we <u>passed</u> a traffic light, the lanes shifted. He was <u>straddling</u> the dotted line that divided two lanes of traffic. "Get in your own lane," I yelled.

Puzzled, he looked at me. "Which one is mine?" he asked.

With this crisis over, we came to a traffic light that was yellow and about to turn red. My brother stopped the car in such a hurry that the tires squealed.

By now he was a bit shaken. He sat at the light, catching his <u>breath</u> and looking around. He did not <u>notice</u> when the light changed to green, then yellow, red, green, yellow, and back to red.

At this point, a policeman walked up to the car and <u>tapped</u> on the window. "That's all the colors we've got around here, boys," he said.

SPELLING BOX:	1. passed	2. straddling
3. breath	4. notice	5. tapped

25. Using Interesting Language

(There is more than one acceptable way to enliven this piece. Accept all reasonable variations.)

It was a gorgeous day. The weather was sunny and warm. It couldn't have been any prettier if it had been custom-ordered. What a great day to spend outside!

A six-year-old boy was playing outside. He skipped down a winding path to a small creek with sparkling water. He chose some flat, round stones to skip across the water. Next, the boy rolled up his blue jeans and waded gingerly into the cold water.

He was having great fun exploring along the mossy banks of the creek. Seeing some movement in the tall grass, he peered down curiously. There he found a small, green frog.

The frog stared back at him, then croaked, "Kiss me and I will turn into an unbelievably beautiful princess."

The small boy examined the frog. Without a word, he put the frog in his pocket and continued his explorations.

The frog demanded loudly, "Hey, why didn't you kiss me?"

"Silly frog," the boy laughed. "I'd rather have a talking frog than a dumb old princess any day!"

SPELLING BOX:	1. temperature	2. weather
3. creek	4. carefully	5. quietly

26. Avoiding Wordiness

(There may be more than one acceptable way to correct these sentences. Accept any reasonable answers. Below is an example.)

The 20-year-old reporter had just started his first job as a cub reporter for a major newspaper in Dallas, Texas.

The young reporter was hardworking and produced accurate, absorbing, and well-written stories.

But there was one problem. His stories were always much too long to fit in the space the newspaper could allot.

His editor talked to him several times with no effect. On this day, the editor called him in again and said, "You don't listen to me. I see I must repeat myself. I think your stories are too long. You must keep your copy short. For your next story, please include only the bare facts. Eventually you'll get it."

Later that day, the reporter was reassigned to report on a train accident. He turned in this copy:

"B. Sampson walked out onto the subway tracks to see if the train was coming. It was. Age 42."

SPELLING BOX:	1. beginning	2. accurate
3. effect	4. bare	5. eventually

27. Making Comparisons Correctly

A woman had inspected the merchandise in every department in the (largest, most largest) department store in town. She liked to dress (good, well). She knew she looked (good, well) in blue, but she couldn't decide which was (more, most) attractive of two blue blouses. She needed slacks (bad, badly), so she looked at many pairs, but she couldn't choose which was (better, best). Shoes were on sale; she looked at pair after pair declaring each one (uglier, ugliest) than the last. She found a coat she liked better than (any, any other) coat. The store didn't have the (most prettiest, prettiest) coat in her size. That was the (more, most) disappointing of all!

She moved on to the cosmetics department. The scent of the cologne was (most, more) overpowering than (the perfume, the perfume's). This store carried more brands than (anyone, anyone else). The light floral scents were the (most, more) appealing of all the scents. But the woman couldn't decide if she liked the lily or peach scent (better, best). Both smelled (good, well). She felt (bad, badly) about not choosing anything to buy.

The woman continued to the housewares department. Of all the departments in the store this was her (favorite, most favorite) because this store had the (better, best) selection in town. The prices were (less, least) expensive than the other (store, stores'). She picked up and examined (more, most) of the items in the linens department.

Then she browsed in the china section. Two china patterns looked (good, well), but she couldn't choose which would go (better, best) in her home. The crystal was the (less, least) economical choice of all the items in that department.

So she continued throughout the store. By the end of the day she had handled more items than (any, any other) customer in the history of the store. Finally, a manager approached her. "Ma'am, I feel (bad, badly) for asking, but are you shopping here?"

"Certainly," she replied in a surprised tone. "What else would I be doing?"

"Well, ma'am," he replied. "I thought perhaps you were doing an inventory."

SPELLING BOX:	1. merchandise	2. disappointing
3. choose	4. history	5. approached

28. Correct Usage

Caroline had been working at the same office job for quite (a while, awhile). The job was (alot, a lot) of work, and there were (fewer, less) benefits every year (accept, except) a fairly reasonable paycheck. (Irregardless, Regardless), Caroline (couldn't hardly, could hardly) stand to go to work every day. It was an (all together, altogether) unsatisfactory situation. She could see little choice (besides, beside) looking for a new job.

Caroline decided to (proceed, precede) with her job search. She hoped she could find something different (from, than) what she (all ready, already) had. Caroline wrote her resume on her computer. She listed her (past, passed) experience. She wrote a cover letter that she hoped would have a positive (affect, effect) on prospective employers. She proofread the letter (good, well). Then she signed it "(Respectively, Respectfully) yours."

Caroline e-mailed her letter to dozens of potential employers. She attached her resume to each one. Since the job market was good, she hoped she would get several good offers (among, between) which she could choose. But she had far (fewer, less) offers than she expected; in fact, after two weeks had (passed, past) she had none at all! She couldn't imagine what could (of, have) gone wrong. She certainly didn't want to (emigrate, immigrate) to another country to find a job!

Finally, she received a message from one of the prospective employers. (That there, That) message explained why her efforts hadn't gone (further, farther) toward landing her a job.

The message (said, says), "Your resume was not attached to your letter as stated. However, I was pleased to (accept, except) your delicious recipe for chocolate fudge cake!"

Spelling Box:	1. benefits	2. unsatisfactory
3. computer	4. hoped	5. employers

29. Review I

(Answers may vary. Accept any reasonable revisions of these problem sentences.)

1. Try to avoid splitting an infinitive.
2. Don't be wordy.
3. It is not necessary or appropriate to use a lot of foreign words.
4. Use specific nouns and verbs to make your writing more interesting.
5. Don't use double negatives.
6. Avoid the use of dangling and misplaced modifiers.
7. Verbs and their subjects must always agree.
8. Proofread your writing carefully to find careless errors and to see if you left words out.
9. Good writers do not shift their point of view.
10. This usage rule, unlike many others, is never to be broken.

Spelling Box:	1. superfluous	2. extraneous
3. unnecessary	4. foreign	5. errors

30. Review II

(Answers will vary. Accept any reasonable revisions.)

A teacher was reviewing that week's vocabulary words with her class. She said, "I think that each of you needs to study your words more. On last week's test you got fewer correct than I would like to see. So, let's go through the words."

"Mike, use the word 'income' in a sentence," she began.

"I open the door and income the dog," Mike replied.

"Gio, try the word 'information,'" she continued bravely.

Gio said, "The fighter jets flew information."

The teacher sighed but went on. "Miko, please use the word 'gruesome' correctly."

"That's easy," Miko replied. "I was pretty short last year, but this summer I gruesome."

"Biswa, try the word 'adverb,' please."

"An adverb is a verb that likes to do math," he answered.

"No, no, no!" shouted the teacher. "Let's try the easiest one. Jane, the word is 'décor.'"

"No problem," said Jane. "D'core is what's in the middle of d'apple!"

Spelling Box:	1. reviewing	2. vocabulary
3. correct	4. easiest	5. problem

31. Review III

Norm came home after his first day of school. His father met him at the door and asked, "How did you like going back to school today?"

Norm said, "Oh, going was all right, and coming home was fine, too. It was the in-between part I didn't like. Dad, will you please help me with my homework? I have something for every subject. For science, I have to write a paragraph about nitrates. It must be turned in tomorrow."

"Well, that's easy, son. When you call long distance they're cheaper than day rates!" Dad replied.

"I also have to look up the law of gravity. It keeps us from falling off the earth," Norm said.

"That should be interesting. But I forget: What kept us from falling off before the law was passed?" Dad answered.

"I don't know," said Norm. "Now, I also have to write an autobiography for English. It should be one page long. It is due next Tuesday."

"An autobiography is a car's life story. Look one up on the Internet," Dad said.

"I also need to prepare some information on whether or not television will take the place of newspapers."

"Of course it won't!" said Dad indignantly. "Did you ever try to kill a fly with a rolled up television?"

"For history I need to know something about the Iron Age," Norm continued.

His dad replied that he was sorry, but he was a bit rusty on that one. (**no quotation marks**)

"To top it all off, in math I have to find the common denominator," Norm said.

"Well, my boy, they must have really lost it. They were looking for it back when I was in school," Dad said.

SPELLING BOX:	1. distance	2. they're
3. off	4. passed	5. whether

32. Review IV

(Answers will vary. Accept all reasonable revisions.)

Gary, a sophomore at Belhaven College, was planning to fly home for Thanksgiving break. Since the day before Thanksgiving is one of the busiest flying days of the year, he was buying his tickets a month in advance. It was a harder job than he thought. There were a lot of choices to make.

He had the choice of calling a travel agent, calling the airlines directly, or using the Internet to search for fares. It was easier to use the Internet to compare fares. First of all, he had to choose which days to leave and return. It made a big difference in the fare. Tuesdays, Wednesdays, and Saturdays were the cheapest days to fly. Sundays were the most expensive.

Next, he had to choose the time of day. The 8:00 A.M. and 5:00 P.M. flights were more money; that was probably because these flights were more popular with business travelers.

He also had to choose if he wanted a direct flight. The ones with stops were a little less money, and that was important since he was on a tight budget.

Gary's eyes became tired as he sat at his Dell computer. Nonetheless, he kept on entering choices, trying to come up with the best deal. When he found a ticket for $99, Gary made the purchase, putting it on his MasterCard.

Arriving at Jones International Airport on the day of the flight, Gary had the choice of the close-in parking lot at $15 per day or the cheap lot with the shuttle bus for $7 a day. He chose the latter. He rushed to the Delta Airlines ticket counter, where he had to choose a window, aisle, or middle seat.

Settling into his narrow seat, he was approached by the stewardess shortly after takeoff. She asked, "Would you like to have a meal?"

"What are my choices?" he replied.

"Yes or no."

SPELLING BOX:	1. sophomore	2. choose
3. fare	4. travelers	5. aisle

33. Review V

(Answers may vary. Accept all reasonable revisions.)

It was a beautiful spring morning. The sun was shining, and the sky was blue. Several wispy, white clouds were floating lazily in the air. The daffodils, as well as a tulip, were poking their heads out of the ground. The grass was getting green, and many of the trees were beginning to leaf out. Each of the birds in the yard was singing its finest song. It was altogether a very fine morning.

The previous week had been spring break. All of the students were granted an entire week off from school. The weather had cooperated, and everyone had enjoyed being outside in their yards or out at the lake.

But now it was Monday morning and time to go back to school. The return to classes, books, and homework was something no one looked forward to. But now the dreaded day had arrived.

A mother walked into her son's room. She said, "Time to get up and go to school!"

"But I don't want to," said the son. Pulling his pillow over his head, he went back to sleep, and the bed became still again.

Once again, the mother came into the room. All was dark and still. Looking at the bed, she saw a big lump in the middle.

"You must get up," the mother insisted. "You'll be late."

"But everyone hates me," replied the son. "Not one person in that entire school likes me. Neither the teachers nor the students like me. They all try to avoid me. When they see me coming, they turn and go the other way. Not only that, the food in the cafeteria is lousy."

The mom listened to all this as long as she could stand it. "Be that as it may," she said finally, you have no choice. You have to go. You're 35 years old, and you're the principal."

SPELLING BOX:	1. daffodils	2. beginning
3. altogether	4. You're	5. principal

34. Review VI

(Answers will vary. Accept all reasonable revisions.)

A city man was driving down a country road about 50 miles from Salt Lake City, Utah. It was a beautiful area near the Wasatch Mountains. He had read about this scenic drive in the best-selling book Round the Mountain by Sheila B. Cumming, and he had been looking forward to it for a long time.

Suddenly his car sputtered to a stop near a field where a herd of cows was grazing. He looked at his instrument panel; neither the gas nor the oil was low. He got out the official owner's manual entitled Keeping Your Car Running by Ira Fuse. Finding nothing helpful in the book, he decided to check the tires.

The man opened the hood and peered in at the engine, but nothing seemed wrong. Then he noticed a cow from the large herd was watching him.

"I do believe it's your radiator," said the cow.

The man was surprised. He ran to the nearest farmhouse and knocked on the door. It was opened by an old farmer. "One of your cows just gave me advice about my car," the man shouted to the farmer.

The farmer leaned against the door. "The cow with the two big brown spots on her side?" the farmer asked. (Rewritten to avoid wordiness.)

"Yes, yes, that's the one!" the man excitedly replied.

"Oh, that's Ethel," said the farmer. "Don't pay attention to her; she doesn't know anything about cars."

SPELLING BOX:	1. scenic	2. herd
3. neither	4. radiator	5. advice

35. Review VII

(Answers will vary. Accept all reasonable revisions.)

It had been a long, hot, dry summer in the Rocky Mountains of the western United States. Wildfires were breaking out daily across the region. Some were ignited by careless campers, others by lightning striking tall lodgepole pines. The fire that was later named "The Willie Fire" was caused by a lighted cigarette thrown out the window of a car traveling down the Cooke City Highway. The fire spread quickly, soon threatening to overrun the small town of Red Lodge, which was nestled in a mountain valley.

Major newspapers, magazines, and television networks rushed reporters and photographers to the scene. Each of these media was billing "The Willie Fire" as their top news story of the week.

When the first photographer arrived in Red Lodge, he saw that the smoke was so thick he could not shoot pictures of the firefighters from the ground. However, he was able to hire a plane.

It was a short drive to the grassy field that served as the town's airport. He saw a small Cessna plane warming up, and he ran and jumped in. He told the pilot to take off. Within a few minutes they were airborne.

The photographer asked the pilot to turn west and make low circling passes over the area where the firefighters were fighting the fire. He, like all good photographers, was hoping to get some good shots of the firefighters in action.

"Why?" asked the pilot.

"Because I'm a photographer. I need to take pictures. I have my Kodak film loaded and my Nikon camera ready for action."

The pilot looked stunned; in fact, he was speechless. Finally, he stammered, "You mean you're not my flight instructor?"

SPELLING BOX:	1. breaking	2. cigarette
3. valley	4. stammered	5. you're

Find the Errors! II *Posttest*

(Answers may vary. Accept any correct revisions.)

1. The Algebra II class of Forest Hill High School, a well-known Maryland school, visited the U.S. Mint in Philadelphia, Pennsylvania.

2. There are many Spanish-speaking Americans in the Miami area, so many signs are printed in both English and Spanish (for example: "Stop!" and "Para!").

3. Our new street address is unusual; it is 333 33rd Street (a lot of 3's).

4. I saw my brother's new blue jacket, which he had lost last Wednesday, hanging on a peg.

5. The fifteen-year-old girl, as well as her two brothers, goes to Washington High School, and they are hardly ever on time to school in the morning.

6. The running back carried the football fifty yards, slid across the goal line, and scored the winning touchdown.

   OR The running back carries the football fifty yards, slides across the goal line, and scores the winning touchdown.

7. The little girl was scared when she lost sight of her mother in the store.

8. William and Lydia are getting married, and they are planning a honeymoon at the beach, which they both love.

9. Luis and Marta are on the cross-country team; they both like to run sprints.

10. Eudora Welty, a famous writer born in Jackson, Mississippi, wrote novels and short stories.

11. I think that I need to redo that job.

12. Thomas Edison was one of the world's best inventors; the lightbulb was one of his most useful inventions.

13. The dog has already eaten its dinner and is lying on the floor under the broken table.

14. My science paper, which I titled "Effects of Light on Plant Growth," did well in the science fair, and everyone liked it.

15. In his book Tales from Margaritaville, Jimmy Buffet said, "It takes no more time to see the good side of life than to see the bad."

Misspelled words: There, Wednesday, running, winning, sight, inventors, already, its, lying, everyone.

Posttest Error Analysis

1. capitalization, commas, abbreviations, hyphens
2. capitalization, usage, hyphens, commas, spelling
3. apostrophes, semicolons, capitalization
4. misplaced modifier, apostrophe, commas, spelling
5. hyphens, capitalization, double negative, commas, subject-verb agreement
6. consistent verb tense, commas, spelling
7. unclear pronoun reference
8. sentence fragments, commas
9. semicolon, run-on sentence, hyphen
10. combining short, choppy sentences; commas
11. avoiding wordiness
12. correct comparisons, apostrophes
13. usage, spelling
14. quotation marks, usage, commas, correct comparisons, capital letters, spelling
15. underlining, quotation marks, capitalization, commas

Activities

Capitalization
Student Exercises 1 and 2

1. Go through the capitalization rules on pages 40–41 with the class. Write examples of troublesome rules on the board and challenge students to add proper capitalization.

2. Have students write announcements about an upcoming event, either real or imaginary. The announcement should include the name of the event, time, date, place, location, etc. Have students exchange announcements and check to see that capitalization is correct and all needed information has been provided.

3. Challenge students to list (using proper capitalization) proper nouns in each of these categories: persons with titles, ethnic groups, national groups, languages, organizations, institutions, political parties, businesses, monuments, buildings, bridges, brand names, documents, awards, laws, countries, continents, states, counties, cities, bodies of water, streets, planets, directions, ships, planes, trains, spacecraft, historical events, calendar parts, religious terms, school courses, and titles of works such as stories, poems, books, etc.

4. Have students write sentences using proper adjectives correctly.

5. Have students write a paragraph about a place they would like to visit. They are to tell about the sights they would like to see. Have them use at least 15 proper nouns and adjectives in the paragraph.

6. Have students work in groups to construct travel brochures to convince visitors to come visit their town. In the brochure, they should describe all the desirable features of their town including sights, parks, amusements, colleges, etc. They should use as many proper nouns and adjectives as possible.

7. Have each student illustrate a different capitalization rule from pages 40–41 on poster board. Encourage humor and creativity on the posters.

8. Divide the capitalization rules among the students. Ask them to find usage examples of their rule(s) in newspapers or magazines. Make a bulletin board display of the rules and examples.

9. Have students draw their own imaginary island. They should name at least 10 geographical features on the island, using proper capitalization.

10. Have students write a brief report on the life of a famous African American, using as many proper nouns as possible.

11. Have a "capitalization bee." Divide the class into two teams. Call out words to each team alternately. Have a student tell whether the word should be capitalized and give the rule that applies.

Commas
Student Exercises 3 and 4

1. Discuss the rules for using commas found on pages 41–42. Write troublesome rules on the board and give examples of following each rule correctly.

2. Have students write original sentences illustrating each of the rules for the use of the comma.

3. Divide the class into two teams. Write a sentence on the board to illustrate a tricky use of the comma. Ask the first team to correctly punctuate the sentence. If the team is correct, it scores a point. Write another sentence and ask the second team to punctuate it. The first team to score 5 points wins.

4. Have students work in teams. Each team is to produce 10 sentences that should be punctuated by one or more commas. They are to write their sentences, leaving out the commas. The teams will then exchange sentences and try to correctly punctuate each other's sentences. The group that adds the most commas correctly wins.

5. Have students write original paragraphs on a topic of their choosing. The paragraph should contain at least 10 correct uses of the comma.

6. Have students invent their own community of the future and write a descriptive essay about it. They should include at least 10 examples of commas used correctly.

7. Have students write paragraphs about famous Hispanic Americans. They should include at least 10 examples of commas used correctly.

Quotation Marks
Student Exercise 5

1. Explain the rules for using quotation marks found on page 42. Write examples of troublesome sentences on the board and discuss them.

2. Have students write a one-page dialogue between two people discussing their plans for the summer vacation.

3. Have students write five pairs of sentences showing correct use of direct and indirect quotations.
   Examples: Laderean said that he would go with us.
   Laderean said, "I will go with you."

4. In a newspaper or magazine, find an interesting photo of two people talking. Have students write an imaginary conversation between the two. Check for correct use of quotation marks. Students may wish to read their conversations aloud.

5. Have students write a dialogue between two friends deciding what they'd like to do on Friday night.

6. Allow students to work in groups. Have them rewrite a dialogue scene from a play or TV show using their own words. They should take care to use the proper form for writing a dialogue.

Hyphens, Colons, and Semicolons
Student Exercise 6

1. Explain the rules for using hyphens, colons, and semicolons found on page 43. Write examples of troublesome sentences on the board.

2. Assign students to use the dictionary to look up rules for dividing words into syllables correctly. Have them report their findings to the class.

3. Have students write a business letter using the correct format. In the letter, they should use at least one hyphen, one semicolon, and one colon.

4. Have students write one sentence using each rule on page 43 for hyphens, colons, and semicolons correctly (a total of 16 sentences).

5. Have students read e.e. cummings' poem "in just-," in which the poet uses hyphens to create images in unusual ways.

Apostrophes
Student Exercise 7

1. Explain the rules for using apostrophes on page 43. Write examples of troublesome sentences on the board.

2. Divide students into teams of two. Have each student write a note to the other student on the team. They are to use at least 10 words with apostrophes in the note. Have students exchange notes and then check all the words containing apostrophes to see that they are correct.

3. Have students write a motivational speech in which they attempt to persuade others to join a campaign or project (e.g., volunteer work, recycling project in the school). In the speech, they should use at least 5 possessives and 10 contractions.

4. Call out words that can be made into contractions and have students take turns spelling the contraction forms (e.g., Call out "do not" and a student spells "don't").

5. Write singular and plural nouns on the board. Have students write the possessive forms. Examples to use include: everybody, one, each other, it, woman, man, class, box, cities, streets, men, Smiths, children, editor-in-chief, somebody, sister-in-law, the Beatles.

6. Have students take turns writing sentences containing plural words, symbols, and words referred to as words on the board.
   Example: She misspelled all the *its* and *it's* in her paper. (words referred to as words)

7. Write a letter to the editor of your school newspaper. Use at least 10 words containing apostrophes in the letter.

Parentheses
Student Exercise 8

1. Explain the rules for using parentheses on page 44. Write examples of troublesome rules on the board.

2. Have students write one example of each rule. Have volunteers come to the board to write their sentences for the class to check.

3. Write sentences using parentheses on the board. Make some sentences correct, some incorrect.

Have students take turns telling why each sentence is correct or incorrect.

Italics, Underlining, and Quotation Marks
Student Exercise 9

1. Explain the rules for using italics/underlining on page 44 and the rules for quotation marks on page 42. Write examples of troublesome rules on the board.
2. Have students write a paragraph in which they tell about their favorite movie, song, book, poem, magazine, newspaper, short story, and television series. They should use italics (underlining) and quotation marks correctly.
3. Have students write a paragraph telling about an article they have read in a magazine. They should give the full name of the article and magazine.
4. Have students write sentences on the board using foreign words. Discuss whether the foreign word should be underlined or not. (Underlining and italics should not be used if the word is commonly used.)

Numbers and Numerals
Student Exercise 10

1. Explain the rules for using numbers in writing found on pages 44–45. Write examples of troublesome rules on the board.
2. Have students write a paragraph describing a sporting event (real or imaginary). They should use as many numbers as possible including (for example): the score; number of people attending; numbers of hits, baskets, goals; new records set; score at halftime, quarter, etc.
3. Have students write a paragraph describing a home or building, using as many numbers as possible. For example, they may give dimensions, number of rooms, number of bathrooms, etc.
4. Have students write a paragraph about a mathematical process or a scientific experiment.
5. Have students write sentences illustrating each rule for using numbers in writing.

Abbreviations
Student Exercise 11

1. Explain the rules for using abbreviations on page 45. Write examples of troublesome rules on the board.
2. Have students write sentences using each rule concerning abbreviations.
3. Have students write paragraphs on a subject of their choice using as many different types of abbreviations as possible. See who can use the most abbreviations correctly in a single paragraph (no more than one page). The student who has the most abbreviations may read her paragraph aloud, writing the abbreviations on the board or spelling them.

Subject-Verb Agreement
Student Exercise 15

1. Explain the rules for avoiding subject-verb errors on pages 45–46.
2. Have students write sample sentences on the board that illustrate correct or incorrect uses of the rules. Other students may guess whether each sentence is correct or not.
3. Have students write sentences using compound subjects. They should be sure the subject and verb agree in each.
4. Have students write one sentence to illustrate each rule on pages 45–46.
5. Have students write a paragraph on a famous Asian American, making sure that all subjects and verbs agree.

Principal Parts of Verbs
Student Exercise 16

1. Explain the rules for proper use of principal parts of verbs on page 46.
2. Have students divide a piece of paper into columns. Title one column "Regular Verbs" and the other "Irregular Verbs." They are to write as many verbs as they can think of that fit into each category. This is a good cooperative learning activity.
3. Create more sentences using problem verbs. Have students complete the sentences correctly.
4. Have students write a short story in which they use as many verbs as possible. They should

underline each regular verb once and each irregular verb twice.

5. Divide the class into two teams. Write sentences on the board that illustrate sets of problem words (e.g., lie, lay; rise, raise). Choose a member of the first team to complete the first sentence. If the answer is correct, that team scores a point.

Consistent Verb Tense
Student Exercise 17

1. Explain the rules for avoiding verb tense shifts on page 46.
2. Have students write a sentence first in present tense, then in past, then in the future. Have students explain when each sentence would be used.
3. Have students write a narrative paragraph about something they did last week. Check the papers for consistency of verb tense.
4. Write sentences which contain a shift in verb tense on the board. Have students correct these.
5. Have students volunteer to write sentences with verb tense shifts on the board. They may call on another student to correct the sentences.
6. Assign students to write a narrative essay about something that happened in elementary school. Have them check for consistency of tense.

Case of Personal Pronouns
Student Exercise 18

1. Explain the rules for choosing correct pronouns found on pages 46–47. Write examples of troublesome rules on the board.
2. Write a list of compound subjects containing one or more pronouns on the board. Have students write original sentences using each compound subject.
3. Have students write five original sentences using compound subjects containing one or more pronouns.
4. Have students write five original sentences using compound direct objects or indirect objects containing one or more pronouns.
5. On the board write *its, it's, their, they're, your,* and *you're.* Have students write sentences in which they use these words correctly.
6. Challenge students to find examples of *its, it's, their, they're, your,* and *you're* used incorrectly

in newspaper, signs, ads, etc. They should bring these examples to class.

7. Have students write a paragraph about a famous Native American, being sure to use pronouns correctly.

Pronoun-Antecedent Agreement
Student Exercise 19

1. Explain the rules for making pronouns and antecedents agree, found on page 47. Write examples of troublesome rules on the board.
2. Have each student write three sentences that contain a pronoun and antecedent. Ask for volunteers to write their sentences on the board. The class may check for pronoun-antecedent agreement in number and gender.
3. Have students write a sentence using each of the following indefinite pronouns:
   a. (always singular) *anybody, anyone, anything, each, either, everybody, everyone, everything, neither, nobody, no one, nothing, one, somebody, someone, something*
   b. (always plural) *both, few, many, several*
   c. (singular or plural) *all, any, most, none, some*

Clear Pronoun Reference
Student Exercise 20

1. Explain the rules for clear pronoun references on page 47. Write examples of troublesome rules on the board.
2. Have students write sentences containing vague pronoun references (*this, that, which,* and *it*) or ambiguous pronoun references. Ask for volunteers to write their sentences on the board and call on a classmate to come forward to correct each sentence.

Dangling or Misplaced Modifiers
Student Exercise 22

1. Explain the rules for avoiding dangling or misplaced modifiers on page 47. Write examples of any troublesome rules.
2. Have students think of humorous examples of sentences with dangling or misplaced modifiers. Ask for volunteers to write their sentences on the board or read them out loud.

3. Have students construct posters containing humorous examples of sentences with dangling or misplaced modifiers. They should write each sentence on a poster, then illustrate the mistaken meaning the reader of the sentence might get.

4. Have a student come to the board and write an introductory phrase such as: *Avoiding the water, Finishing the paper, Screaming loudly.* That student may call on another student to come forward and complete the sentence sensibly.

5. Have students work in teams to come up with humorous sentences containing dangling or misplaced modifiers. Share these with the class.

Sentence Fragments and Run-on Sentences
Student Exercise 23

1. Explain the rules for avoiding fragments and run-on sentences on page 48. Write examples of any troublesome rules on the board.

2. Read aloud a mixture of fragments and run-on sentences. Have students tell how many sentences they hear (0, 1, 2, 3 . . .) and explain their answer.

3. Write a paragraph on the board with no punctuation. Have students copy the paragraph and punctuate it correctly.

4. Write a mixture of fragments and short sentences on the board. Do not punctuate any of these. Call on students to tell which are fragments and which are complete sentences. In the case of a sentence fragment, students should tell which part of the sentence is missing.

5. Write a list of sentence fragments on the board. Students are to use each fragment to make a complete sentence.

6. Have students write a paragraph on a topic of their choosing in which they use at least five compound sentences punctuated correctly to avoid run-ons.

Varying Sentence Styles
Student Exercise 24

1. Explain the rules for varying sentence style found on page 48. Write examples of troublesome sentences on the board.

2. Have students write paragraphs in which they vary the length of their sentences, vary the kinds of sentences they write, and vary the beginnings of the sentences. Correct their paragraphs, pointing out any of the rules for Exercise 23 that have not been followed.

3. Write a paragraph on the board in which every sentence is short and choppy. Have students rewrite the paragraph, adding details if needed to make a more interesting paragraph in which sentence length and style are varied.

Using Interesting Language
Student Exercise 25

1. Explain the rules on pages 48–49, writing examples of any troublesome rules on the board.

2. Have students write a descriptive paragraph using specific adjectives and nouns that give a clear, precise picture.

3. Have students write a descriptive paragraph using specific verbs to give a clear, precise picture of something a person is doing (a sport, an activity . . .).

4. Make a list of overused, boring adjectives and verbs on the board. Have students brainstorm more interesting words that could be used. Examples of overused words: *nice, pretty, bad, go, look, say, fine.*

5. Divide the class into two teams. Write a boring adjective (such as *nice*) on the board. Have the teams work together for five minutes to see how many alternative words they can think of. Have them read their lists aloud.

6. Write some words naming general categories on the board. Examples: food, shelter, clothing, entertainment, people, animals, etc. Students are to write the category words across the top of their paper. Then they are to list specific, interesting words under each category. See how many words they can list in 10 minutes.

7. Write a short, boring sentence on the board. Call on different students to give more interesting sentences using this sentence as a base.
   Examples: A man walked his dog.
   A little old man walked a huge St. Bernard.

8. Choose a picture from a magazine or from your textbook. Have students write a descriptive paragraph about the picture using interesting words. Call for volunteers to read their paragraphs aloud.

9. Have students write a descriptive brochure about your town or school. They are to use lively, interesting vocabulary to make the place they choose sound interesting and inviting.

Avoiding Wordiness
Student Exercise 26

1. Explain the rules for avoiding wordiness on page 49. Write examples on the board of troublesome rules.
2. Write examples of wordy sentences, sentences using double negatives, etc., on the board. Have students rewrite them correctly.
3. Ask for volunteers to write wordy sentences on the board for other students to correct.

Making Comparisons Correctly
Student Exercise 27

1. Explain the rules for making comparisons correctly on pages 49–50. Write examples of troublesome sentences on the board.
2. Have students write a paragraph in which they compare three or more animals in as many ways as possible. They should use words containing

-*er* or -*est* or the intensifiers *more* and *most* plus an adjective or adverb.
3. Write sentences using illogical comparisons or incomplete comparisons on the board. Ask students to come to the board and correct the sentences.
4. Write sentences that would contain *good* or *well* on the board, leaving a blank where the proper word should go. Have students fill in the correct word.

Correct Usage
Student Exercise 28

1. Explain the guidelines for correct usage on pages 50–51. Write examples of troublesome sentences on the board.
2. Have students construct pairs of sentences using the words on pages 50–51 correctly.
3. Write sentences using the words on pages 50–51 on the board. Have students tell whether the words were used correctly.
4. Have students write paragraphs in which they use as many of the words on pages 50–51 as possible.

Spelling Box Word List

Numbers in parentheses are lesson numbers.

a lot (pretest)
abated (1)
acceptable (23)
accurate (23, 26)
achieve (17)
admit (17)
admitted (22)
advice (1, 34)
aisle (32)
all right (16)
all together (pretest)
allowed (5)
almost (3)
already (posttest)
altogether (33)
amateur (22)
angrily (18)
announced (11)
apology (21)
applicant (14)
appointment (5)
approached (27)
approximately (20)
arctic (8)
argument (19)
assistant (12)
author (pretest)
babies (36)
bare (26)
beginning (26, 33)
benefits (28)
binoculars (22)
breaking (35)
breath (24)
campaign (22)
carefully (25)
century (pretest, 10)
chief (1)
chivalry (14)
choose (27, 32)
cigarette (35)
comedian (20)
commercials (9)
complaining (17)
complaints (7)
computer (28)
confusion (4)

correct (30)
counselor (5)
course (4)
courteously (36)
creek (25)
cruise (13)
daffodils (33)
dear (12)
desert (8)
deserted (15)
difference (10)
dilemma (19)
disappear (2)
disappearing (15)
disappointing (27)
distance (31)
due (13)
easiest (30)
effect (26)
embarrassed (16)
embarrassing (12)
employers (28)
entirely (15)
environment (13)
errors (29)
essential (3)
eventually (26)
everyone (posttest)
excellent (19)
except (pretest)
extraneous (29)
extremely (15)
fare (32)
favorite (6, 9)
foreign (29)
forgotten (6)
forty (15)
furious (18)
hammer (7)
herd (34)
history (27)
holes (11)
hoped (28)
hundred (10, 23)
immediately (21)
independently (3)
insecticide (1)

instructor (2)
interested (6)
inventors (posttest)
it's (5)
its (posttest)
labor (3)
latter (pretest)
leak (11)
license (13)
lightning (6)
literature (9)
litter (13)
lively (9)
lobby (36)
lounging (18)
lying (posttest)
may be (pretest)
mayor (2)
merchandise (27)
misspelled (14)
mosquitoes (1)
motor (7)
neither (34)
nonsense (11)
notice (10, 24)
noticeable (16)
occasion (8)
off (31)
overboard (19)
package (18)
passed (pretest, 24, 31)
past (36)
peace (7)
perfect (21)
personal (16)
personnel (14)
piece (17, 36)
plane (21)
planning (9)
practical (19)
principal (33)
principally (8)
priorities (8)
problem (30)
professional (20)
professor (11)
quietly (25)

radiator (34)
realized (20)
recognize (6)
recommended (3)
refrigerator (pretest)
relieved (5, 14)
reluctant (4)
replied (20)
reviewing (30)
running (posttest)
scenic (34)
schedule (17)
secretary (18)
service (16)
shoe (10)
sight (posttest)
skies (23)
sophomore (32)
stammered (35)
stare (2)
straddling (24)
success (4)
suddenly (23)
superfluous (29)
tapped (24)
tapping (7)
temperature (25)
temporarily (4)
their (pretest)
there (posttest)
they're (31)
travelers (32)
unaccustomed (12)
unnecessary (29)
unsatisfactory (28)
vacuumed (21)
valley (35)
veil (22)
vocabulary (30)
weather (25)
Wednesday (posttest)
weight (2)
whether (31)
windshield (12)
winning (posttest)
you're (33, 35)